Restoring the
Anglican Mind

Middleton presents his case eloquently and thoughtfully … an excellent work … read it.

Bishop Alec Graham, *Church Times*

There is a measured passion in the writing that commands respect and needs to be taken seriously and requires engagement from those who seek to pursue a different course of action …

William Davage, *Parson and Parish*
– the journal of the English Clergy Association

He brings all his learning and his keen intelligence and clear thinking to this book … the breadth of his reading is distilled, his command of his material in such a narrow compass is astonishingly compelling.

Alexander Fawdon, *New Directions*

This persuasive book … finishes with an excellent Agenda for Action, not, it's true 39 articles in number, but they're as worthy of attention as their predecessor.

Alan Edwards, *Church of England Newspaper*

This book contains many gems which clarify our thoughts. It is an essential read for all who are involved in the life and work of the Church.

John Pitchford, *Forward Plus*

This significant book is essential reading for everyone concerned about the Church of England.

Margaret Laird, *Church Observer*

Restoring the Anglican Mind

Arthur Middleton

GRACEWING

First published in 2008
Reprinted 2009

Gracewing
2 Southern Avenue,
Leominster
Herefordshire HR6 0QF

ISBN 978 0 85244 695 9

Front cover: St Augustine of Canterbury © Aidan Hart

Typeset by Action Publishing Technology Ltd,
Gloucester GL1 5SR

Contents

Illustrations

Foreword

With Anglicanism in turmoil in America, on the march in Africa and bewildered here in England the Anglican Association is thankful for the opportunity to welcome this second edition of a widely acclaimed book. Accordingly I warmly commend Canon Arthur Middleton's book to you. It is both a thoughtful and a robust defence of Anglican orthodoxy.

Canon Middleton, a significantly published theologian, is always a resolute and ready champion of that which is right and true and wise in these matters. As well as being a theologian of very considerable ability he had the benefit of having been for many years a parish priest – which has, in turn, kept him in touch with those in the pew. He has always been someone who has asserted in his Anglicanism a 'catholic integrity' which is 'patristic rather than papal'. In this book he sees his aim as proclaiming 'a western Orthodoxy'.

Just before his 'Afterword' the author gives us an Agenda to follow and he ends this book with an incisive summary of what has followed the events of Summer 2008 and what must now happen in the period before us.

It has seemed to me that the Church of England has tended to give far more thought to policies than it has to principles. It is true that a Christian culture cannot be static but excessive change can be a sign of spiritual and intellectual confusion rather than deepening insight. Of course we can see today some matters that may not have been clear generations ago. However there are basic beliefs that do not change and cannot be altered without huge damage.

What is more, we would all fare better if promises were kept rather than broken. The voting majority at the July 2008 meeting of the Church of England's General Synod behaved disgracefully in overturning assurances given to everyone less than two decades ago. The lack of consensus which is plain for all to see begs the question as to whether a Synod that has only a five year life-span has (or should have) the right to alter irrevocably the future shape and doctrine of the Church. Such a change would fly in the face of centuries and centuries of history – and belief.

Neil Inkley, a friend of mine from Preston in Lancashire, wrote elsewhere: 'It is, sadly, ironic that, as my mortgage has long since been paid off, the chances that my house will be repossessed in these troublesome financial times are small; but the chances that my Church will be repossessed begin to look extremely high'. He added that there are those 'who will be satisfied only when there is no roof over my head'.

This must not be allowed to happen.

Canon Middleton in the pages that follow explains why orthodox Anglicanism is essential to our whole religious experience. He takes us back to first principles and shows us how they still speak to us today. We need to see how the peculiar character of the Church of England deserves to be studied and understood.

At the moment the Church of England seems to be 'floating its currency'. Yet if we read Middleton's wise words set out here we will have a firm base for steadying the ship. The same must be true for Anglicans across the world – in Provinces 'beyond the Seas'.

Take the time to read the chapters that follow including, of course, the *Afterword* which brings the story right up-to-the-minute.

These wise words give pause for thought and a clear idea of the concerns we must confront in the period ahead.

Anthony Kilmister
President, The Anglican Association

Restoring the
Anglican Mind

Richard Hooker

1

Vision and Wholeness

When, as Rector of Boldon I stood on the Chancel steps of the church, a Saxon foundation dedicated to St Nicholas of Myra, I faced east to say the Nicene Creed. Before me were two Byzantine mosaics, one of St Nicholas who attended the Council of Nicaea and opposed the Arians who reduced Christ to the Son, created not begotten, and the other of St George, on each side of the East Window that depicts Van Eyk's *Adoration of the Lamb*. It is a typical thirteenth-century English Chancel that was added to a church built by Benedictine monks from Wearmouth and Jarrow. As we said those words proclaiming the Nicene faith – *God of God, Light of Light, Very God of Very God, Begotten not made, Being of one substance with the Father. By whom all things were made. Who for us men and for our salvation came down from heaven; And was incarnate of the Holy Ghost of the Virgin Mary, And was made man* – there was a wonderful sense of convergence, a harmony in these words and sights of the Christian East and West

Such sights open the door to a spirituality that fulfils a deep, religious need. They are worthy of a place in our Christian worship because of their contemplative qualities as their form inspires serenity and their content invites meditation. Their content is determined by the Holy Scriptures and the tradition of the Church expressing true teaching in visual form just as preaching is expressed verbally. St John Damascene pointed out that just as words encourage hearing, so do images stimulate the eyes, making for a fundamental equivalence between words and images, between theology and these Christian art forms of East and West Like Scripture and tradition they are conveyors of divine revelations, one of several mediums the Church uses to communicate the Gospel.[1]

Here in Boldon it is the Church of England expressing its kinship with the apostolic faith and order of the One Holy Catholic and Apostolic Church, in the architecture and history of continuous worship initiated by the Anglo-Saxons, continued by the Benedictines, with their roots in Cassian and the Desert Fathers. In these mosaics, in two Russian icons above a Chantry altar, the icons of the Nativity, Christ's Baptism and Christ enthroned as the True Vine, we see no ill-conceived juxtaposition of traditions, nor an eccentric orientalising of Anglicanism. These are the many associations of orthodox Christianity in which nothing is out of place.

Catholicity and Apostolicity

This scene that was before me as I celebrated the daily Liturgy of Eucharist and Office focuses in a tangible way a conviction that has guided my spiritual pilgrimage throughout my ministry as a priest in the Church of England: that the Christian East and West can, and must, discover again that fundamental synthesis of perspective that characterised the ancient, undivided Church. Far from being a pious hope, I believe it to be fundamental to

---

[1.] Solrun Nes, *The Mystical Language of Icons* (Canterbury Press, 2004), p. 13.

our faithfulness to the Gospel and vital in the Church's challenge to the world. This vision is no idiosyncrasy but is endemic to Anglicanism, and has been since the Reformation because Protestantism in Anglicanism (unlike the direction taken by some of the other Reformers), was a quest for Catholicity. For the Reformers as for the Fathers, Catholicity was a theological and historical concept before it was a geographical and statistical one. The essence of such Catholicity lies in faithfulness to the gospel word and sacramental usage given to the Church by Christ through the Apostles from the beginning, so that Catholicity is a matter of apostolicity and apostolicity primarily a matter of doctrine. The Reformers are concerned with the maintenance of Catholic doctrine and institution, the re-establishment of biblical faith, which, they were convinced, had been preserved in the early Christian Fathers, who had been faithful expositors of it. Thus the Catholic integrity of Anglicanism is patristic rather than papal. As E. Charles Miller Jnr points out:

> The particular character of the Anglican settlement – with its interplay between Scripture, tradition, and reason, together with its constant, if sometimes clumsy, will, to profess only the faith of the undivided Church – has fostered a proximity with Orthodoxy which cannot be ignored. The history of Anglican thought abounds with examples of those who have seen in the East an uninterrupted expression of this same synthesis which became the peculiar gift of Anglicanism.[2]

H. A. Hodges and *A Western Orthodoxy*

Over fifty years ago the philosopher and theologian H. A. Hodges wrote his essay *Anglicanism and Orthodoxy* and

---

[2.] E. C. Miller Jnr, *Towards a Fuller Vision* (Moorhouse Barrow Wilson, 1984), p. 2.

expressed the conviction that Anglicanism is uniquely called to be the embodiment of Orthodoxy in the West This was no naive call for Anglicans to start wearing chimney pot hats and to grow beards. It was a daring cry for a judicious and explicit expression of an indigenous orthodoxy in terms of the life and thought of western peoples,

> ... coming with all their western background, their western habits and traditions, into the circle of the Orthodox Faith. Then we should have an Orthodoxy which was really western because its memory was western – a memory of the Christian history of the West, not as the West now remembers it, but purged and set in perspective by the Orthodox Faith.[3]

He sees this as enriching Eastern Orthodoxy, setting it free from its merely ethnic and parochial character by giving it a more universal and Catholic perspective. It will not be a matter of reconstituting the western experience in a new and alien cosmetic, but learning to possess the western inheritance in a new way, by discriminating 'the vein of error in what we have hitherto found convincing, and to possess the whole in thankfulness and penitence'.[4] For Hodges this embodying of a Western Orthodoxy is the vocation of Anglicanism, which also for this author is essential, if to make a theology means to make more and more truly one's own, by experience, the mystery of the relation of God to Man that has been traditionally lived by the Church. This is what we find in the theology of the seventeenth-century Anglican divine Lancelot Andrewes, whose originality was described by the Eastern Orthodox theologian Nicholas Lossky as consisting, not so much in innovation, as in enabling the whole era to grasp the

---

[3.] H. A. Hodges, *Anglicanism and Orthodoxy* (S.C.M., 1957), p. 52.

[4.] *Ibid.*, p. 53.

genuine essence of the Christian message. This is consistent with how Hodges sees the possibility of embodying this Western Orthodoxy. It requires a vigorous decision 'not to become identified with any special form of doctrine over and above that of the whole undivided Church, and not to let the papal autocracy be replaced by an oligarchy of Biblical theologians and preachers of the Word'.[5] Anglicanism's concern is for a balanced synthesis between Scripture, tradition, and reason, a discovery of which, for Hodges, would be 'Western Orthodoxy at last made visible'.

For many Anglicans this balanced synthesis is not part of their experience, yet in the history of Anglicanism numerous divines have encountered in themselves the convergence of East and West, put succinctly by Lancelot Andrewes in his *Private Devotions*, where he prays 'for the whole Church Catholic, Eastern, Western, our own'. Some have their doubts about the interaction of two streams of tradition that for centuries have developed in such seemingly different ways. The criticism often made is that orthodoxy has not had to deal with the particular issues that have shaped and challenged western Christianity. While this evaluation may be correct, Miller points out that

> ... this gives the Orthodox a unique and potentially invaluable perspective on our western situation. Precisely because they speak objectively, from without, they may be able to offer evaluations and insights after which we in the West could only grope. To think that their vibrant tradition, shaped, as we must suppose, by the prompting of the Holy Spirit, is of little or no use to the life and thought of western Christianity is an affront to the Gospel dictum that 'they may all be one'. [John 17:11.].[6]

---

5. *Ibid.*, p. 56.
6. *Ibid.*, p. 4.

Gareth Bennett

2

The *Crockford's Preface*

The hysteria surrounding Gareth Bennett's *Crockford's Preface* (1987–88) caused many to miss its most important point. In a section entitled 'A Theology in Retreat', he pinpointed the crisis within Anglicanism as being fundamentally theological and stemming from a deliberate rejection of this balanced synthesis. For Bennett, the most significant change in contemporary Anglicanism is the decline of a distinctive Anglican theological method. This had been identified by the great divines of the seventeenth century as giving attention to Scripture, tradition and reason to establish doctrine.

> The context of such theological study was the corporate life of the Church and the end was to deepen its spirituality and forward its mission. Such a view of theology appears in official Anglican reports and in archiepiscopal addresses. But the last real exponent of classical Anglican divinity was Archbishop Michael Ramsey whose many scholarly studies represent a last stand before the citadel fell to the repeated assaults of a younger generation of academics. The essential characteristic of the new theologians lies in their unease in combining the role of theologian and churchman, and their wish to study both Scripture and the patristic age without reference to the apologetic patterns of later Christianity ... Such a distancing of the modern Church from what had been regarded as its prescriptive sources clearly has serious consequences for Anglican ecclesiology, and this has been help-

fully set out in Mr. J. L. Houlden's book *Connections* (1986). Here he quite specifically rejects the notion of 'living in a tradition.' It would seem that modern man must live amid the ruins of past doctrinal and ecclesiastical systems, looking to the Scriptures only for themes and apprehensions which may inform his individual exploration of the mystery of God.[1]

The preface was about the nature and identity of modern Anglicanism, a serious analysis of the malaise of the Church of England in particular, and of Anglicanism, at least in Anglo-Saxon countries in general; that it has become deeply secularised which means that it has become deeply committed to the assumptions and values of the present age. Anglicanism has lost direction because it has ceased to be Anglicanism. The only viable alternative is to return to our own roots and learn from tradition.

> ... the disappearance of the Prayer Book and the collapse of the traditional Anglican way of doing theology are intimately connected. Prayer and doctrine are closely bound up in the Anglican tradition: *Lex orandi, lex credendi* (which means that the rule of prayer governs what we believe) ... the way a Church does its thinking about God in the end tells us what kind of Church it is; here we will read its character, however dry and over intellectual such an approach may at first seem. It may be, indeed, that the very fact that Anglican theology has in recent years taken such matters out of the normal ambit of ordinary believers says more about Anglicanism's current sickness than anything else.

For, in the end, thinking about God and praying to him are only seen as radically different activities when something has gone wrong; when they separate out completely (as in much modernist theology) what has occurred is something like the curdling of mayonnaise. Thus, when Bennett reminds us in the preface of the familiar triangular formula identifying the Anglican method as 'giving attention to Scripture, Tradition and Reason to establish doctrine,' he goes on to emphasize

---

[1.] G. Bennett, *Preface to Crockford's Clerical Directory 1987–88* (CIO).

that this is no merely cerebral activity: 'the context of such theological study' he insists, 'was the corporate life of the Church and the end was to deepen its Spirituality.'[2]

Gareth Bennett is not the first voice to highlight this crisis. Dr Eric Mascall, in a chapter entitled 'The Contemporary Crisis',[3] cited numerous people such as Canon Smyth who commented that academic theologians gave the impression of belonging to a debating society preoccupied with textual criticism and philosophy, while in the parishes where the real battle for the faith was being fought, the Church 'amid much discouragement combats materialism and indifference'.

Mascall claimed that 'theology' in the proper sense of that term – the study of God and his creatures in relation to him – 'is now in imminent danger of becoming virtually extinct'. Professor N. P. Williams, the Lady Margaret Professor at Oxford, warned of this in 1933, contrasting theology as it had been understood in its grand period and as it was already coming to be in his own time. It had ceased to mean the science of God; its contents consisting in the cardinal ideas of the Christian religion and in the faculties of modern universities had become 'the science of men's thoughts about God'. Williams concluded that the classical meaning of theology must be content to find a home in theological colleges, which in the light of what contemporary theological education has become is a pipe-dream. In a series of articles based on his Ph.D. research into Regional Theological Courses, the Revd Dr John Edmondson commented:

> The problem, which exists with regard to general academic theology on Regional Courses has a number of facets which are

---

2. William Oddie, *The Crockford's File, Gareth Bennett and the Death of the Anglican Mind* (Hamish Hamilton, 1989), pp. 116–17.
3. E. Mascall, *Theology and the Gospel of Christ, An Essay in Reorientation* (SPCK, 1977), ch. 1, pp. 15ff.

worthy of note. In the first place, if our bishops rate the Courses so lowly in their teaching of theology, it is rather surprising that they are content that the situation should remain unimproved. After all, what is a priest if not a theologian? Surely the understanding and interpretation of the knowledge of God is central to all ordained ministry. Secondly, the teaching of traditional doctrine has been squeezed in all theological institutions because of extra introductions to the curricula, but with the time constraints on the Courses, the problem is made especially acute. Courses stress their emphasis on the inculcation of a pattern of life-long learning, but the contrasting survey results tend to imply that students graduating from the Courses may not be fully aware of the magnitude of the corpus of theology they have yet to espouse, as against that which they have enjoyed touching upon. At interview, more than one Course Principal used the phrase 'scratching the surface' in connection with describing the task in hand.

Finally there is the question of theological approach. There is not now the prevailing degree of liberalism that there once was on Courses, but Anglo-Catholics and Evangelicals alike still report instances of that intolerant liberalism among lecturers which is ready to ridicule the holding of orthodox views by students as simply untenable in the context of contemporary theological education. The Courses have a remit of catering for students from the whole spectrum of churchmanship but, because of low staffing levels, each student is likely to find only one member of staff who understands him or her fully.[4]

The effects of contemporary theological education are summarised in *Believe it or Not! What Church of England Clergy Actually Believe*, a survey carried out by Christian Research in 2002. It concluded;

This Survey has finally exposed what many Anglicans of various traditions have long suspected: the existence side-by-side of two separate churches under the cloak of Anglicanism.

[4.] Dr John Edmondson, 'Water Board Theology', in *New Directions*, May 2004 (original emphasis).

One of these is essentially credally orthodox and committed to the historic faith and Apostolic mission of the Church; the other is wrapped in the garments of Christian language, but has only the most tenuous grasp of the central teachings of the faith ... It has clearly demonstrated that despite the much-vaunted diversity within the Church of England, such diversity is due to the existence *of two churches with irreconcilable theological beliefs and moral values.*

Their divergence has often been portrayed as being solely concerned with the issue of the ordination of women as priest and bishop – but this is no more than the *presenting symptom* of the many insoluble divisions which must arise from radically different attitudes to the authority of Scripture, the doctrines of Creation and Incarnation and, most critically, the person of Jesus Christ.

This Survey reveals the divisions are far wider and go much deeper than any single presenting symptom. Conservative evangelicals and Catholics, for all their historic differences, hold in common both the faith and the traditional moral teachings of the undivided Catholic Church. Liberals, by contrast, embrace a theology and moral methodology deriving from the prevailing views of the secular society in which they live. Conformist rather than prophetic, they appear to have little interest in transforming the world by the grace of a Saviour about whose claim upon their lives they are deeply uncertain if not dismissive.[5]

Also, to return to Mascall. He quoted from *The Christian Mind* by Harry Blamires writing in 1963:

It is a commonplace that the mind of modern man has been secularised. For instance, it has been deprived of any orientation towards the supernatural. Tragic as this fact is, it would not be so desperately tragic had the Christian mind held out against the secular drift. But unfortunately the Christian mind has succumbed to the secular drift with a degree of weakness and nervelessness unmatched in Christian history. It is difficult to do justice in words to the complete loss of

---

[5.] Christian Research and Cost of Conscience, 2003.

intellectual morale in the twentieth-century Church. One cannot characterise it without having recourse to language which will sound hysterical and melodramatic ... There is no longer a Christian mind.[6]

Blamires goes on to claim that there is still, 'a Christian ethic, a Christian practice, a Christian spirituality. As a moral being, the modern Christian subscribes to a code other than that of the non-Christian.' Though as Mascall pointed out, if Blamires had been writing ten years later he would have detected an erosion of Christian ethics, practice and spirituality, as well as Christian thinking. Since 1977 when Mascall wrote, the situation has disintegrated far more severely so that one wonders about whether moral theology has become the science about what people think God ought to allow into their behaviour.

In an address to the National Conference of the Prayer Book Society at Trinity Hall, Cambridge on 10 September 1983, Enoch Powell spoke of the dismantling of 'the intellectual and emotional scaffolding of religious observance'.

> The Tractarians were doubly right when they acclaimed the Book of Common Prayer as the proof of the Catholicism of the Anglican Church: right because the words and formulae, being themselves impregnable, were susceptible of an interpretation which bridged the gulf of the Reformation; and right because the essential mark of Catholicism, uniformity imposed by universal authority, was placed upon it by the untrammelled *imperium* of the English nation state. Without the authoritative fixity of its liturgy, the unique comprehensiveness and broadmindedness of the Church of England would not have been possible.
>
> The cause of the Book of Common Prayer is not a literary or an aesthetic cause: it is a religious cause. It lies athwart the religious dilemma of our society, a society not emancipated from the necessities, including the religious necessities, of all

---

6. H. Blamires, *The Christian Mind* (SPCK, 1963).

human societies, but a society where the intellectual and emotional scaffolding of religious observance has been dismantled, not least by the very caste which is specialised in society for sustaining, commending and interpreting it. The deliberate attack upon the Book of Common Prayer which the last decade has witnessed is a conscious and integral part of that dismantling process – inevitably so, because the Anglican Church and its liturgical heritage survive, almost alone since the ravaging of the Roman Church, as living evidence of essential elements in religious experience and expression. I suspect that we who maintain the Book of Common Prayer are fighting in a wider warfare than we can know.

Post-Crockford

So Gareth Bennett is one of a number of twentieth-century Anglicans who saw the theological crisis within Anglicanism. Yet the arrogance and hostility that greeted Bennett's preface was ferocious. Now his words seem singularly prophetic. The unfolding events in the Church of England in particular, and the Anglican Communion in general, exhibit certain resolute principles of change that have not only signalled a departure from that apostolic faith and order on which her claim to Catholicity rests, but also devastated her unity and distanced her further from the One Holy Catholic and Apostolic Church that has effectively stalled ecumenical progress. This is the consequence of revolutionary innovation that has rendered the Church of England in particular and the Anglican Communion in general dysfunctional.

Underlying such innovation is a changed attitude towards the authority of Holy Scripture. Many are now of the opinion that the Bible can guide in some areas of life but not in all. Where it conflicts with current sociological and political presuppositions the innovators ignore it as a relic of a culturally conditioned and antiquated world view. Hence for them the authority of the Bible is questionable and and so too is the teaching of the Apostles and the practice of the Catholic Church through the ages. Gender has ceased to be an issue because the revolutionary changes the innovators seek to inflict upon the Church are matters of human rights and social justice, and Anglicanism today is more enlightened than earlier generations of the Holy Catholic Church in discerning what God's Church needs. The guidance of the Holy Spirit is what frees us from the past and enables our thinking and actions to be consistent with the will of God. The proponents of such innovations see themselves as being 'prophetic' and will resist all opposition in their determination to implement them and demonstrate the rightness of their views. It was obvious in the debate on women bishops in General Synod in 2006 and the response of the House of Bishops to Cardinal Kasper's warnings in 2006 on behalf of the Pope, as well as those of the Patriarch of the Orthodox Church, that most Synod members do not want to listen to theology. In their arrogance they believe that the rest of the Anglican Communion, with the Orthodox and Roman Churches, will catch up with them when they see the wisdom of their new insights.

The same innovatory principles lie behind the current controversies over the ordination and consecration of practising homosexuals and blessing same-sex relationships that is tearing the Anglican Communion apart. The same principles were used to justify the ordination of women to the priesthood and episcopate, the start of the slippery slope, when it was prophesied that they would become the justification of the homosexual lifestyle. They have been used to legitimise abortion and the divorce culture. Will euthanasia be next? What is happening was described by Gareth Bennett as 'a retreat from theology'. A close examination of the principles will reveal that several run contrary to classical Anglican Formularies, and others reveal nothing more than Anglo-American arrogance, even an Anglican arrogance, and the fact that the Church of England has too readily and uncritically been influenced by the American Episcopal Church.

The scenario for the General Synod vote in November 1992, to allow women to become priests, to feminise apostolic priestly order, can be traced to 1973 when these principles clearly emerged at the General Convention of the American Episcopal Church in Louisville. Despite a decision not to authorise the ordination of women to the priesthood, and in defiance of it in July 1974, eleven female deacons were ordained as priests in Philadelphia. This contravened the Constitution and Canons of the Episcopal Church. Nevertheless, American Episcopalians were persuaded to see these ordinations as prophetic rather than defiant and by a very slight majority voted to change the canons to allow the ordination of women as priests and bishops.

> The result has been a failure of authority, and the subsequent breakdown of communion ... Classical Anglicanism, of course, knows no such thing as Provincial Autonomy. The Prayer Book and Articles are designed to hold the church together, not to allow it to drift apart. Whereas in minor matters Diocesan Bishops are permitted to settle local arguments, and when necessary to have them resolved by the Archbishop, that would certainly not be the case when part of the church decided to alter the basis of ordination to the priesthood or the episcopate. Article 34 ... says that 'every particular or national church hath authority to ordain, change and abolish ceremonies or rites of the Church ordained only by man's authority, so that all things be done to edifying'. This identifies a particular church – a title which Roman Catholic theology applies to a diocese – with a national church. It gives no support to theories of Provincial, or Diocesan authority, such as is claimed increasingly in the 'Anglican

Communion' (another construct of which classical Anglicanism is blissfully ignorant).[7]

The same step was taken with the Canons of the Church of
England.

> ... with the passing of legislation in 1992 aimed at women's
> ordination to the priesthood a new item of canon law was
> introduced in the form of Canon C4B. Though its effect was
> and is devastating, the text of C4B is 'deliciously' simple. It
> reads:
> 1. A woman may be ordained to the office of a priest if she
>   otherwise satisfies the requirements of Canon C4 as to the
>   persons who may be ordained as priests.
> 2. In the forms of service contained in the Book of Common
>   Prayer or in the Ordinal words importing the masculine
>   gender in relation to the priesthood shall be construed as
>   including the feminine, except where the context otherwise
>   requires.

> Those two paragraphs amounted to the placing of an *erratum*
> slip in the Prayer Book so that, after 300 years, the BCP could
> be understood differently and with ambiguity. The words on
> the page in the Prayer Book Ordinal could be taken to mean
> one thing or equally to mean another thing according to
> taste.[8]

Kilmister continued with a point about the preface to the
BCP:

> That Preface, composed by Bishop Robert Sanderson of
> Lincoln, is in no doubt in declaring the Church's deliberate
> intention to preserve the inherited catholic order which has
> been the guarantee of its continuing identity. Of course the
> ordination of women within the Church of England has

---

7. Edwin Barnes, *Authority: Who Says So? An Examination of Authority in the Church of England* (Tufton Books, 2006), p. 14.

8. Anthony Kilmister, *The Prayer Book and Ordination* (Tufton Books, 2006), p. 24.

already severely tested any claim of the Church to be *continuing* the Order found in the 'ancient Authors'. No-one can reasonably claim that women-priests are part of a continuation of the Orders to which the 'ancient Authors' were referring. The happenings of the Nineteen-Nineties are a 'politically correct' discontinuation or innovation.[9]

In November 1992 the General Synod passed by a slender majority a motion to permit the ordination of women. This was far from being a consensual vote and is responsible for wide-spread disunity in the Church of England. By sleight of hand, the service for the Ordering of Priests was shown to require *only* (!) re-interpretation. But the Synod's action has pushed back by decades the ecumenical achievements of the last century signifying that the Church does not actually believe in 'that they may all be one'. Furthermore the introductory passage in the Prayer Book headed *Of Ceremonies*[10] makes it clear that the breaking of a common Order is no small offence before God.

It was asserted that the change was only implemented because it was understood that the ordination of women would be permissive only, never mandatory, and no bishop or diocese, we were assured at the time, would ever be forced to adopt this innovation which was not only contrary to the theology of holy order embedded in our Formularies and the BCP, but held by many in our own Church. Also, it flew in the face of the Roman Catholic Church and the Orthodox Churches with whom we were actively pursuing ecumenical discussions such as the Anglican Roman Catholic International Commission (ARCIC), where the discussion of holy order was on the agenda. Needless to say, there are many horror stories of opponents, clergy and laity, being bullied by bishops and

---

[9.] *Ibid.*, p. 25 (original emphasis).
[10.] *The Book of Common Prayer* (Everyman's Library 1999), p. 11.

archdeacons and pressurised to rescind resolutions taken for legal protection under the Act of Synod and the Provincial Episcopal Visitor, 'the flying bishop'. Furthermore we were told that the matter of women's ordination had not been finally settled because we were in a period of 'reception.' The actions of some diocesan senior staff, who acted as if the acceptance of such ordinations was mandatory, violated the consciences of clergy and laity alike. Further, the *Pilling Report* (2007), which is an enquiry into the way in which senior appointments are made, has openly admitted that there is bias against the appointment to high office of opponents to women priests.

In America and in this country, as a result of the devastation unleashed by the 1976 Convention and the 1992 General Synod respectively, individuals and whole parishes began to leave the Church into which many of them had been born and which they loved. Some became Roman Catholics or joined the Orthodox Church. Others joined the Continuing Anglican Churches which sprang up, and some – particularly in America – put themselves under the authority of an African Primate, while others gave up being part of the Church.

Despite such assurances, the principles of revolutionary change outlined here are deeply rooted in the American Episcopal Church (ECUSA) and they are emerging in the Church of England, holding both in an apparently unbreakable, vice-like grip. They are the operative principles behind many of the actions of some of our bishops and others – since 1976 in America and 1992 here in England. It should have been no surprise when in 2003 the American General Convention agreed to consecrate as a bishop a divorced man living in an active homosexual partnership. Also, there was in ECUSA an unvoiced approval towards the ongoing practice of priests and bishops publicly endorsing homosexual conduct and blessing homosexual relationships. In 1977 a pastoral letter in America had stated that 'this Church confines its nuptial blessing to the union of male and female', and that the bishops 'agree to deny ordination to an advocating and/or practicing homosexual person', arguing that, 'In each case we must not condone what we believe God wills to redeem.' Nevertheless, the gay-rights lobby continued its unrelenting assault on the American Episcopal Church with the single aim of forcing the acceptance of homosexual 'orientation' and homosexual conduct, and to demand that such conduct be blessed by the Church. As a result the 2003 Convention consented to the consecration of a man who in an earlier time would have been deposed for immorality. The Episcopal Church had been seduced by the orchestrated propaganda for 'gay rights,' which was not concerned with holy order or Christian morality but with what they defined as human rights rather than God's will for his Church.

Is it not surprising because one of the 'Philadelphia Eleven' illegally ordained to the priesthood in 1974, Carter Heyward, was a practising lesbian. She was described in an Episcopal News Service article on 10 September 1981 as 'an openly avowed lesbian priest on the faculty of the Episcopal Divinity School in Cambridge, Massachusetts who has done much to speak out for justice for gay/lesbian people in the Church and elsewhere'. Also, she concelebrated at the consecration of Bishop Barbara Harris in 1989. So the seeds of this ideology, intent on revolutionary innovation that is destructive of apostolic faith and order, have been germinating long before 2003 and the controversial consecration of Gene Robinson as Bishop of New Hampshire in 2003.

It should be obvious that there is a connection between the principles used to justify the ordination of women as priests and bishops and the justification for homosexual priests (and bishops) and for homosexual 'marriage.' The same is happening in the Anglican Church in Canada. What has happened is that socio-political ideology seeded and germinated and thereby supplanted the scriptural norms of Christian theology and morality in the mind-set of North American Anglicans. It is now dividing the Anglican Communion with the African and Global South Anglicans calling for the Communion to distance itself from this ideology. In the book *To Mend the Net*, they set out their proposals for the disciplining of erring provinces but were given insufficient encouragement. They have threatened to boycott the 2008 Lambeth Conference unless North American Anglicans recant their stance on homosexuality, and are calling for American Anglicans to be excluded from attendance if they refuse to do so. The threat may well be withdrawn by the time of the Lambeth meeting.

Applying Ancient Precedent

The African and Global South Primates have also acted to combat the heterodox doctrine and morality that is being promoted by the American Episcopal Church, by offering Primatial and Episcopal oversight to dioceses leaving the American Church; and they have ordained orthodox priests and consecrated orthodox bishops to minister within them. Their actions have been condemned as violating jurisdictional boundaries. Too often the crisis has been reduced to a political or jurisdictional matter that is the business of structures and quasi-authoritative bodies focused in the Lambeth Conference or the Anglican Consultative Council (ACC) and Primates summit meetings. Yet, as Gareth Bennett's *Crockford's Preface* stated, 'no-one should underestimate the capacity of a Lambeth

Conference to take its real decisions by doing nothing.'
What seems to happen is that what Bennett claimed was
Spong's understanding of Anglican comprehensiveness,
'that everyone should do what seems right to him in
conscience and that everyone should accept it,' is what
prevails; and Primates are found nailing their colours to
the fence.

Not so with Archbishop Akinola and the Primate of the
Global South. Their concern was to combat the heterodox
doctrine and morality that is being embraced and promoted
by ECUSA in the liberal interpretation of Scripture and
most recently its pledge, contrary to the resolution of the
Lambeth Conference, to provide 'support, encouragement
and pastoral care to homosexual relationships' and same-
sex blessings. There was even more concern about
ECUSA's willingness to tolerate wide-ranging viewpoints
on the truth of the Gospels and the divinity of Christ Episcopacy is not only about communion in jurisdictional structures because apostolic succession is not just about a line of
succession in persons. There must also be continuity and
succession in matters of faith and order, in the truth of the
Gospel and in the apostolic ministry of Word and Sacrament. Where this truth of the Gospel is compromised there
can be no communion and unity in truth and holiness. The
fundamental problem is doctrinal before it is political and
jurisdictional and so as bishops they stand under the
authority of 'the faith which was once and but once and for
all delivered to the saints' and in which they have pledged
themselves to drive away all false and erroneous doctrine.
Anglicanism has always claimed that in faith and order the
Anglican Communion is continuous in identity with the
Primitive Church. In fact, in the Book of Common Prayer, in
the Preface, Canons and Formularies it claims the Primitive
Church as its model. Canon A5, *Of the doctrine of the Church
of England* stipulates that:

The doctrine of the Church of England is grounded in the Holy Scriptures, and in such teachings of the ancient Fathers and Councils of the Church as are agreeable to the said Scriptures. In particular such doctrine is to be found in The Thirty-nine Articles of Religion, the Book of Common Prayer, and the Ordinal.[11]

The *Windsor Report* published in October 2004 called for moratoria on the ordination of practising homosexuals and the promotion of rites for blessing same-sex partnerships. Also, it called on traditionalist bishops to abandon their intervention in the dioceses of 'revisionist' bishops, and required both traditionalist and revisionist groups to express regret for their actions, as incompatible with the bonds of communion. Bishop Tom Wright of Durham defended the report's censure of this action of orthodox Anglican bishops.[12] In an article in *The Tablet*, a Roman Catholic publication, he claimed that such interventions were 'in contravention not only of Anglican custom but of the Nicene decrees on the subject'. This has given rise to a theory of the inviolable integrity of diocesan boundaries, the consequence of such a theory being that 'heresy is preferable to schism' and 'schism is worse than heresy' where diversity is exalted above doctrinal and moral unity.

Professor Tighe states that the bishop went further during an interview with *Christianity Today*, and asserted that such violations of diocesan boundaries are prohibited by the Council of Nicaea 'because that's not how episcopacy works'. Then he contended that 'the real charge' against revisionist dioceses is the unilateral implementing

---

11. *The Canons of the Church of England* (SPCK, 1969), pp. 3ff.
12. For a full discussion of this see Professor William Tighe's article, 'Abusing the Fathers, *The Windsor Report's Misleading Appeal to Nicaea'*, *Touchstone*, April 2005 (http://touchstonemag.com /archives/author.php?id=123).

of innovations that lacked the proper theological rationale and due regard for the rest of the communion. In his mind the bishops and archbishops intervening in other people's provinces and dioceses are, in effect, at that level, guilty of the same error. There is a failure in the bishop's reasoning to grasp the 'mind of the Fathers' concerning heresy. It was the *Rule of Faith* and the *consensus patrum* that distinguished between true and false doctrine and not one individual bishop judging another bishop in a Spong-like individualism that understands Anglican comprehensiveness where everyone should do what seems right to him in conscience and everyone else should accept it. In the Early Church a bishop guilty of heresy would cease to be a bishop and the see considered vacant. As Tighe points out, none of the twenty canons of the Council of Nicaea have any relevance to the situation of the Anglican Communion today.

Antiquities of the Christian Church

Between 1708 and 1722 Joseph Bingham (1668–1723), an Anglican priest and notable patristic scholar, produced his ten-volume work, *Antiquities of the Christian Church*. It is not a mere catalogue of information but a compendium of critically-evaluated evidence for the living tradition of patristic church life. In the two-volume edition of this ten-volume work he discusses '... the Office of Bishops in relation to the whole Catholic Church':

> ... there is yet a more eminent branch of their pastoral office and care behind, which is, their superintendency over the whole catholic church; in which every bishop was supposed to have an equal share, not as to what concerned external polity and government, but the prime, essential part of religion, the preservation of the Christian faith. Whenever the faith was in danger of being subverted by heresy, or

destroyed by persecution, then every bishop thought it part of his duty and office to put to his helping hand, and labour as much for any other diocese as his own. Dioceses were but limits of convenience, for the preservation of order in times of peace; but the faith was a more universal thing, and when war was made upon that, then the whole world was but one diocese, and the whole church but one flock, and every pastor thought himself obliged to feed his great Master's sheep according to his power, whatever part of the world they were scattered in. In this sense, every bishop was a universal pastor and bishop of the whole world, as having a common care and concern for the whole church of Christ This is what St Austin told Boniface, Bishop of Rome, that the pastoral care was common to all those who had the office of bishop; and though he was a little higher advanced toward the top of Christ's watch-tower, yet all others had an equal concern in it.[13]

Cyprian of Carthage[14] testifies that the bishops in his own time were so united that if anyone of the body preached heresy or persecuted the flock of Christ, all the bishops came to its rescue. Gregory of Nazianzus regarded Cyprian as a universal bishop in Carthage and Africa and he speaks similarly of Athanasius. From this came the notion of one bishopric in the Church in which every bishop had a share in the sense that he had an equal concern for the whole. However, in things that did not appertain to the faith they were not to meddle with other men's dioceses, but only be concerned with the business of their own. When the faith or welfare of the Church was at stake, then by this rule of there being one episcopacy, every other bishopric was as much their diocese as their own, '... and no human laws or canons could tie up their hands from performing such acts of their Episcopal office

---

13. Joseph Bingham, *Antiquities of the Christian Church* (Chatto and Windus, 1875), book II, ch. v.
14. *The Ante-Nicene Fathers* (T. T. Clark/Eerdmans, 1986), vol. V, pp. 369–75.

in any part of the world, as they thought necessary for the preservation of religion'.

The rule in the Primitive Church was that no bishop should ordain in another's diocese without his permission and for order's sake this was generally observed. There were exceptions to this rule when a situation demanded that it was necessary to do otherwise. Such situations would be when a bishop became a heretic and would only ordain heretical clergy while persecuting the orthodox. Any Catholic bishop, being a bishop of the universal Church would then be authorised to ordain orthodox men in such a diocese. This was contrary to the common rule, which was waived in such exceptional circumstances for the preservation of the faith. The preservation of the faith is seen to be the supreme rule of all and so the lesser rule had to give way to this superior obligation.

Examples of such exceptions arose when the Church was in danger of being overrun by Arianism. We read of Athanasius[15] having no scruples about ordaining men in cities outside his own diocese. Eusebius of Samosata[16] followed suit. Dressed as a soldier he travelled in Syria, Cilicia, and other places, ordaining men deacons, priests and bishops – Theodoret names them[17] – and putting right whatever he found wanting in the churches.

While this was contrary to the common rule it was necessary for the life of the Church and this is what gave them authority to act as bishops of the whole Catholic Church and exert their power. It is recorded of Epiphanius that he ordained Paulinianus, St Jerome's brother, in a monastery outside his own diocese in Palestine. When

---

15. Socrates History, *Nicene and Post-Nicene Fathers* (T. T. Clark/Eerdmans, 1989), book II, ch. xxiv, p. 520.

16. Theodoret, Ecclesiastical History, *Nicene and Post-Nicene Fathers* (T. T. Clark/Eerdmans, 1989), book IV, ch. xiii, p. 133.

17. *Ibid.*, book V, ch. iv.

challenged that he was acting contrary to canon he vindicated himself on this principle,

> that in cases of necessity such as this was, where the interest of God was to be served, any bishop had power to act in any part of the Church ... Yet the love of Christ was a rule above all: and therefore men were not barely to consider the thing that was done, but the circumstances of the action, the time, the manner, the persons for whose sake, and the end for which it was done.

Two Incompatible Religions

There are emerging in the Anglican Communion two incompatible and competing religions that are not mere differences of 'emphasis,' but profound differences about the content of Christian belief and the character of Christian life. The authority of experience, the basis of liberalism, is set against the authority of divine revelation, fundamental to orthodoxy. For liberalism, belief is a matter of personal opinion based on contemporary experience; an experience in which scripture and liturgy and engagement with various social causes provide data for reflection and change within the Church. Religion then becomes not so much a matter of 'Truth' (with a capital 'T') but of 'truths' that are subject to continual change, revision and adjustment, to make them relevant to contemporary secular culture. The Church in a democratic world must, say the liberals, decide 'truths' by majority vote of representative councils, synods, or other political mechanisms.

For the orthodox, 'Truth' has been definitively revealed in Holy Scripture, and authoritatively interpreted in the Christian tradition. The Christian responds in belief, understanding, and obedience. Relevance is a matter of seeking to apply established doctrinal and moral standards to the situation in which the Church is. Here the Church is divinely commissioned in faith and order, to maintain the faith 'once and for all delivered to the saints', and is responsible for maintaining those standards, essentially unchanged from one age to another. The dividing line is not bold black or white but carries grey areas where some have tried to compromise their accommodation on one side or the other. The Church's mission is to convert the culture, not to be accommodated to it.

A Matter of Authority

Authority is fundamental, resting upon the revelation of God in Jesus Christ that has not been delegated to a consensus in meetings, synods or among bishops. In the absence of an Oecumenical Council the Book of Common Prayer has defined us as Anglicans in worship and provides the basis of our theological method. It has been the standard of doctrine and practice. Anglicans hitherto have held and maintained the Doctrine, Sacraments and Discipline of Christ as the Lord has commanded in Holy Scripture and as the Church of England has received and set out in the Prayer Book and the Thirty-nine Articles.

It would not have occurred to most Anglicans that serious questions of doctrine and worship could be decided by national, provincial or local synods, as the quotation on p. 15ff points out. The Prayer Book tradition was the rock-like standard. Today Liturgy is used to introduce theological changes incompatible with the doctrine expressed in the Prayer Book, making polarisation within the Church sharper and widespread. Laity become demoralised when unable to accommodate to the new religion emerging in their parishes and the parish priest's attitude of 'take it or leave it.' Dean Inge pointed out that a church that is married to the present age is a widow in the next.

Out of date

This new emergent, fashionable religion is out of date in a profound sense because it is theologically inflexible and narrow, expressive of a school of thought which has passed. It has its roots in a variety of attitudes expressed in the theological, social and political movements of the 1960s. These were concerned for the secularisation of the Church, an 'in' word among 'radical' theologians of that time, but with no agreed usage among themselves. For some the issue was largely a matter of the radical re-interpretation of the Gospel. For example Paul van Buren, in his *The Secular Meaning of the Gospel* (1963), thought that the word 'God' is no longer necessary in a secular society; for R. Gregor Smith, *in Secular Christianity* (1966) and *The New Man*, secularisation means a radically new version of the Christian faith as de-supernaturalised. For most of them the idea of secular Christianity is closely bound up with the loss of a worthwhile role for the Christian minis-ter in a technological age. Christians must stop being 'churchy' and pietistic; they must actively concern them-selves with the affairs of secular life. This attitude is often bound up with a denial of the value of corporate worship, prayer and the religious life, and with the passive accep-tance of the death of God as a cultural fact. It represents a radical questioning of the function of the Church and of the role of the minister in social life today. However, Harvey Cox, an American liberal theologian of the 1960s who was passionately concerned for the secularisation of the Church, realised that he got it wrong in *The Secular City*, which means that the secularisation of the Church is expressive of a generation that is passing away. Contemporary developments in the thinking and practice of the Episcopal Church of America and Canada is a variation on this theme, and though the Church of England is a few steps behind them, recent trends in General Synod indicate the presence already of two incompatible religions in England.

St Ambrose

3

Schmemann and A
Return to the Fathers

In his article *Theology and Eucharist* (1961) the late Alexander Schmemann, an American Orthodox theologian, expounded a way in which orthodox theology could overcome its inner weakness and deficiencies by a return to the Fathers. This did not mean repeating what the Fathers had said or the transforming of the thought of early Christianity into a formal or infallible authority or into a body of academic knowledge. This would betray 'the very spirit of the theology of the Fathers'. Schmemann is concerned for the recovery of their spirit, of the secret inspiration which made them true witnesses of the Church.[1] It is not merely a return to texts, abstract tradition, formulas and propositions. The Russian Orthodox theologian Georges Florovsky makes the same point when he says that our contemporary appeal to the Fathers is much more than an historical reference to the past but it is an appeal to the mind of the Fathers and to follow them means to acquire their mind. We return to the Fathers when we recover in our own experience, the Church not merely as an institution, or a system of doctrine, but as the all-embracing, all-assuming and all-transforming Life, the passage into the

---

[1.] A. Schmemann, *Liturgy and Tradition, Theological Reflections of Alexander Schmemann* (ed. Thomas Fisch) (SVS Press,1990), p. 84.

reality of redemption and transfiguration.

> This experience ... is centred in the Eucharist, the Sacrament of the Church, the very manifestation and self-revelation of the Church. Eucharist whether it is expressly referred to or not, is the organic source and necessary 'term of reference' of theology, for if theology is bearing witness to the faith and life of the Church, to the Church as salvation and new life in Christ, it bears witness primarily to the experience of the Church manifested, communicated and actualized in the EuchariSt It is in the Eucharist that the Church ceases to be 'institution, doctrine, system' and becomes Life, Vision, Salvation; it is in the Eucharist that the Word of God is fulfilled and the human mind made capable of expressing the mind of Christ Here then is the source of theology, of *words about God*, 'the event' which transforms our human speculation into a message of Divine Truth.[2]

Bennett and Schmemann Agree

In principle, Bennett and Schmemann agree on the need to return to our roots, to prescriptive sources and to see the corporate worship of the Church as the context of Christian thinking, the source of theology, where theology and experience, intellect and intuition, thinking and praying are kept together. Anglicanism has always sought to keep them together, from the Reformers and the Caroline divines, to Bishop Butler, the Oxford Fathers, F. D. Maurice, William Temple, Michael Ramsey and many others. Their concern was for an ideal of theology which was not divorced from prayer and liturgy, for a way of life and worship informed and structured by theological vision. We have the kind of theology that Schmemann and Bennett are suggesting when we rediscover the Eucharistic character of the Church's life. It is in the Eucharist, that

---

2. *Ibid.*, pp. 84–5 (original emphasis).

experience of the Church as 'the passage into the reality of redemption and transfiguration' where the life of the world to come informs our theology. Indeed, the life of the world to come must be a constant factor in the theological enterpise. This is a patristic perspective (patristic means the spirit of early Christian thought) in which the Eucharist generates the Church's life and informs all aspects of her life. As the theology of Athanasius cannot be understood apart from the liturgy of Bishop Serapion, so the theology of Anglicanism must find its origin and explanation in the Book of Common Prayer. This approach is not alien to Anglicans, for the *appeal to the Fathers* has been a seminal feature of the Anglican theological tradition since the sixteenth century, while the appeal for a more Eucharistic theology in the broadest sense chimes in with the Anglican insistence upon the interaction of theology and worship. The rediscovery of the Eucharist within Anglicanism as a consequence of the Catholic Revival and the Liturgical Movement, both movements being inspired by *a return to the Fathers*, offers us a unique opportunity to recover in a balanced synthesis these dynamics of our tradition, a truly vibrant Christianity that embodies the spirit of early Christian thought and is orthodox in belief and practice.

This could provide a *Western Orthodoxy* as envisaged by Hodges, because Anglicanism is unique in Christendom in having the potential to embody such orthodoxy of faith and practice within a western context. Here we would find important insights for understanding aspects of our Anglican tradition that have been forgotten, or misunderstood, even ignored, in the same way that the Oxford Fathers enabled us to recover forgotten aspects of that same tradition.

The Fathers in Anglicanism

An examination of Anglican roots will demonstrate that the Anglican study of the Fathers was primarily in relation to controversies that Anglicanism had to face in the aftermath of the Reformation and the struggle for Anglican identity, rather than for their own sake. Throughout these controversies it is the Fathers who speak, not only in the defence of Anglicanism, but in defence of themselves and an improper use of their writings. In this sense there is a kinship with the Fathers and the search for Anglican identity, in that it was the controversies of their own times that gave birth to their writings.

Hence Anglicanism has its own peculiar character because in the divines of sixteenth- and seventeenth-century England, in Reformers and Caroline divines, we see something which in one sense is historical but in another sense is of more than historical significance. In these Anglican divines, what is being made present in England is the spirit and substance of that Catholic vision of the mystery of Christ which characterises those early centuries of the Church in East and West This enables us to understand more fully the particular characteristics of the Anglican tradition we have received. Despite the discontinuities of their time these divines are aware of the continuity and wholeness of the Church's tradition in which they lived and for which they worked. Their aim and purpose was to be representatives of the Christian tradition in all its fullness, organic wholeness and unbroken unity. Hence, what we find in their understanding of continuity is no mere mechanical concept. Continuity for them is a dynamic and living transmission of certain living qualities of faith and order, the *tradition*, or to use the Greek word, the *paradosis* that the Church hands on.

Tradition

The authority of *tradition* was first invoked in the second century to counter the heretics' misuse of Scripture. Scripture belonged to the Church and only within the community of right faith could it be adequately understood and correctly interpreted. Heretics were outside the Church and had no key to the mind of Scripture. Citing texts was insufficient, for Scripture was an integrated whole and its meaning could only be elicited by an insight of faith, meaning, not an individualistic insight, but the faith of the Church rooted in the apostolic message and defined as the *Rule of Faith*. Bishop Irenaeus of Lyons in the second century expounded this principle in his *Against Heresies*. This *Rule* is based upon the baptismal formula prescribed by Our Lord in his command to the Church to make all nations his disciples by baptising and teaching (Matthew 28:19, 20). It was the basis of a superstructure comprising the substance of oral instruction communicated by the Lord to his Apostles, *the faith which was once and but once and for all delivered to the saints.* It became the form of Christian instruction to new converts before their baptism, a *Rule of Faith*, a traditional body of doctrine, the apostolic preaching, eventually filled out by the inspired writings of the New Testament. This tradition, became the worldwide test of brotherhood to distinguish the true Christian from heretics, or as Hooker put it, 'a mark whereby to discern Christian men from infidels and Jews.'[3] Irenaeus wrote, 'The Church having received this preaching and this faith, although scattered throughout the whole world, yet, as if occupying one house, carefully preserves it.'[4] It is understood as something received, a primeval tradition,

---

[3.] Richard Hooker, *Laws of Ecclesiastical Polity*, book V, §42.
[4.] Irenaeus, *Against Heresies*, book I, ch. x. 2.

unchanged in substance, from the Apostles.

This tradition has been revealed in Jesus Christ, not as a set of propositions, but as a new life of fellowship between God and man, established once and for all. It makes us 'partakers of the divine nature' and was no human discovery, but a Gospel sent by God through his Incarnate Son. Scripture does not make this possible, but witnesses in a final and complete form to the acts of God which realised it. To be fully understood, the Bible requires the reality of this fellowship that exists in the Church, and into which we are initiated in Baptism when this *Rule of Faith* is handed over to us. So tradition is not just the transmission of inherited doctrines but a continuous life in the truth which is Christ, the sacramental continuity in history of the communion of saints; in a way it is the Church, in which is deposited *the faith once and for all delivered*, which is the primary tradition.

For Irenaeus tradition is the work of the abiding presence of the Holy Spirit in the Church. His whole understanding of the Church is charismatic and institutional, so that tradition in his understanding is something living; a new breath such as was bestowed at creation. Scripture can be rightly and fully understood only in the light and context of this living and apostolic tradition. It was not adding anything to Scripture but providing a living context, 'the comprehensive perspective in which the true "intention" and total "design" of Divine Revelation itself could be detected and grasped'.[5]

The Church then is the 'witness and keeper' of Scripture. We cannot separate the Bible from the Church, because they are two sides of the one Revelation. Bishop Richard Hanson pointed out that the life of the Church depends upon the

---

[5.] G. Florovsky, 'The Function of Tradition,' in *Bible, Church, Tradition, An Eastern Orthodox View* (Nordland, 1972), p. 79.

Church dancing with the Bible, and without each other they are lost;[6] and Fr George Tavard SJ[7] maintained that Anglicanism has always maintained a perfect union between Church and Scripture, more so than the Counter-Reformation theologians of the Roman Catholic Church or the Protestants. Anglicanism has always upheld the view that the Church's authority is not distinct from that of Scripture, but rather that they are one, in the tradition, which is conformable to Scripture. This is the spirit of Irenaeus and the Primitive Church.

Therefore, Anglicanism understands the Church as bearing witness to the *truth*, not by reminiscence or from the words of others, but from its own living, unceasing experience, from its Catholic fullness, which has its roots in continuity with the Primitive Church. This is what constitutes that *tradition of truth* in which the apostolic teaching is not so much an unchangeable example to be repeated or imitated, but an eternally living and inexhaustible source of life and inspiration. Tradition is the constant abiding spirit, not only the memory of words, and is therefore a charismatic not an historical principle, but together with Scripture contains the truth of divine revelation, a truth that lives in the Church. Only within the Church does Scripture live and come to life, being revealed as a whole through the medium of the living experience of the Church. For the Church to be the Church it must be maintained in that truth being 'the Church of the living God, the pillar and bulwark of the truth' (1. Tim. 3:15).

[6.] R. P. C. Hanson, *The Bible as A Norm of Faith: An Inaugural Lecture as Lightfoot Professor of Divinity* (University of Durham: Titus Wilson & Son, 1963), p. 11.

[7] George Tavard, *Holy Writ or Holy Church* (Burns & Oates, 1959), p. 245.

People who stand in this tradition today are called traditionalists. This is an unfortunate word because its use by others caricatures those of us who are people of the Tradition, with a capital 'T,' falsely imprisoning us in the static mode of a past 'golden age' rather than seeing us as twentieth-century people whose lives are rooted in a continuity that is nothing less than the dynamic and living transmission of certain qualities of faith and order. The label is wide of the mark, because we are not fundamentalists in the biblical sense, nor are we 'traditionalists,' for then our sole aim would be an adherence to 'tradition' in a fundamentalist or conservationist manner. If to explain ourselves we need to use labels, we are 'liberal conservatives': liberal in its classical sense of liberality, a generosity of spirit combined with openness in the search for truth, rather than the accommodating mind of the contemporary liberal. We are not holders of the opinions of others that are subject to changing fashions. By being conservative we mean a respect for continuity, treasuring 'tradition,' the *paradosis*, the handing on of the *faith once and for all delivered to the saints*, the best and most durable gifts from the past, where change would be merely formal and not substantial.

Our search for truth is from within a living, not an abstract, tradition that is rooted in the 'faith once and for all delivered to the saints,' and we cannot accept as 'truth' anything that is in plain contradiction to this. This is quite different from being caricatured as resistant to change. It places us in that same tradition as Charles Gore who saw faithfulness to the pillars of Scripture, creed, apostolic ministry and sacraments as the essential conditions for the growth of 'a Catholicism which limits *its* properly dogmatic authority carefully and thankfully by the blessed restriction of Scripture'.[8]

---

[8] C. Gore, *Orders and Unity* (Murray, 1909), p. 200.

Theology in this sense means to make more and more one's own, in the experience of the Church, the mystery of the relation of God to man that has been traditionally lived by the Church. Its originality will consist, not so much in innovation, but in the enabling of the whole era to grasp the genuine essence of the Christian message. The theologian who operates in this way, discovers that the more he penetrates into the heart of the mystery, the more his teaching will be personal and consequently original. Only then will he be able to speak in such a way to his contemporaries that his message will continue to live beyond his time. Of such a quality is the classical theology of Hooker and Andrewes and other great Anglican divines, the essential Anglicanism within which we stand, and in method and content it has much to say to our generation. This is what gives us significance in the present that is crucial for the reintegration of the Church in East and West

John Jebb

4

The Meaning of the
Peculiar Character

Bishop Colin Dunlop claimed that at the Reformation
Thomas Cranmer as Archbishop of Canterbury felt unable
to guide the destiny of the Church of England either along
the road of papal and medieval Latin Christendom, or into
the new pastures of Luther or Calvin. Instead, he set
himself to find traces of that lost thoroughfare of 'the
godly and decent order of the ancient Fathers' but the
English Church remained the Church St Augustine of
Canterbury brought us, while repudiating the authority of
the Pope.[1]

In the English Reformation, the Reformers used the
Fathers chiefly as a means of proving what had and what
had not been primitive doctrine and practice and as a
valuable authority secondary to the Bible. They used the
Fathers in two ways: negatively, to prove the absence of
Roman doctrines; and positively, to promote a right interpretation of Scripture and demonstrate a Scriptural way of
life for the Church. This was not merely embodied in the
opinions of reforming theologians but embedded in such
foundation documents as the Book of Common Prayer, the
Book of the Homilies, the Canons, the Thirty-Nine Articles

[1] C. Dunlop, 'The First Great Figure in Anglicanism', in *Thomas
Cranmer* (Brymill Press, 1989), p. 18.

and the Ordinal. It is all there in those foundation documents. This was significant for the next generation, the Caroline divines of the seventeenth century, who built on the Scriptural theology of the early Fathers, going further than the Reformers in using the thought and piety of the Fathers within the structure of their own theological vision. Their theology finds its centre in the Incarnation, a kinship shared with the Nicene Fathers, and characterised by a vision of the Church that embraces East and West, a consequence of their immersion in Greek and Latin divinity. Again it is a theological vision that is wrought in controversy, in relation to Puritanism and Calvinism on the one side, and Roman Catholicism on the other.

In 1835, Henry Cary published his book, *Testimonies of the Fathers of the First Four Centuries to the Doctrine and Discipline of the Church of England as Set Forth in the Thirty-Nine Articles*. In the preface he pointed out that the principle which especially characterises the Church of England and distinguishes her from every other reformed communion, is her 'marked and avowed adherence to the catholic faith as received in the primitive and purest ages of Christianity'. On this ground, and believing that in the earliest ages the great truths of Christianity were known to, and plainly professed by, the Church, the Church of England (and here he quotes from *The Peculiar Character of the Church of England* by Dr Jebb, the Bishop of Limerick)

> in the first instance, and as her grand foundation, derives all obligatory matter of faith, that is, to use her own expression, all 'that is to be believed for necessity of salvation', from the Scripture alone; and herein she differs from the Church of Rome. But she systematically resorts to the concurrent sense of the Church catholic, both for assistance in the interpretation of the sacred text, and for guidance in those matters of religion, which the text has left at large: and herein she differs from every reformed communion.

Cary laments that this peculiar character of our Church, though known to and commended by learned foreign divines, has 'unfortunately, of late years, been little regarded by the generality of our own clergy'. It is equally true of the clergy today. Yet the roots of this peculiar character of our Church are traceable to the Anglican Reformers of the sixteenth century, who were the first to make the appeal to the Fathers a foundation stone of their divinity, building their theology on patristic dogma, belief and practice. So, to describe Anglicanism as having a peculiar character means that the Catholic faith of the Primitive Church, the faith 'once and for all delivered to the saints', summarised in what is called the *Rule of faith* that is found in Scripture and the Creeds, is the doctrine of Anglicanism. She refuses to affirm as *de fide*, that is, of the faith, any doctrine not so qualified in or by Scripture or the Primitive Church. Jewel affirmed in his *Apologia*, that 'Scripture and the Primitive Church are the criteria by which the authenticity of a Church and the truth of its teaching are assessed', and Bramhall claimed that the Church of England was not 'a new Church, a new Religion, or new Holy Orders'. This constant of the Anglican spirit is found in different shapes from the sixteenth century onwards.

Distinctiveness

Anglican distinctiveness derives from the manner of its theologising and not from the content of its theology. This method emerged with Archbishop Parker's theological interpretation of the Elizabethan Settlement in the 1571 Canons, the Thirty-Nine Articles, the Second Book of Homilies and the 'Canon of Preaching'. Rooted doctrinally in Scripture and antiquity, we find this method in the works of Anglican divines and in our Formularies.

Richard Hooker articulated it in his *Laws of Ecclesiastical Polity*, and Michael Ramsey describes its spirit as '... doing theology to the sound of church bells', to stress the essential connection between theology, doctrine and Christian worship. The Book of Common Prayer is as much about a way of doing theology as about liturgy – *Lex orandi est lex credendi* – which means that it is the law of prayer that determines belief, so that Anglican theology cannot be understood apart from the Book of Common Prayer.

For Hooker, God's revelation in Christ and the Church, the *Whole Christ*, is authoritative, but the language in which it is expressed is not infallible. In essence it is rational but mysterious, defying exact definition. Lancelot Andrewes put it succinctly: 'One canon ... two testaments, three creeds, four general councils, five centuries and the series of the Fathers in that period ... determine the boundary of our faith.'[2] Such an understanding of divine revelation does not deny God's presence in creation. C. S. Lewis noted that Hooker's universe was 'drenched with Deity', and the implications of the divine presence in his world keeps together things that can easily be set in opposition:

> ... reason as well as revelation, nature as well as grace, the commonwealth as well as the Church, are equally though diversely 'of God' ... all kinds of knowledge, all good arts, sciences and disciplines ... we meet in all levels the divine wisdom shining out through 'the beautiful variety of things' in 'their manifold and yet harmonious similitude' ...[3]

This divine presence is one in revelation and nature,

[2.] L. Andrewes, *Works, Opuscula* (Library of Anglo-Catholic Theology, 1841–54), p. 91.
[3.] A. M. Allchin, 'Trinity and Incarnation in Anglican Theology,' in *The Kingdom of Love and Knowledge* (DLT, 1979), pp. 97ff.

consistent and reasonable, in revelation bringing to a climax what God does in nature and in nature giving us the clue to revelation, because 'The Word' that 'became flesh . . .' is the Word or *Logos* at work in all creation. So the Incarnation becomes central and primary to Anglican theology.

Scripture, Tradition, Reason

Anglicanism is neither Cranmerianism nor Hookerianism. Hence, Michael Ramsey could claim that it was the nature of Elizabethan theology rather than imitation of Hooker in the style of Lutherans to Luther or Calvinists to Calvin that made it possible to appeal creatively to Scripture and tradition and it must remain so today. Scripture is the supreme authority because it contains all things necessary to salvation, but not as regulations for everything in the Church's life which has authority to decree rites and ceremonies. Our Formularies affirm the Old Testament revealing Christ by pointing to him and the New Testament revealing Christ fulfilling what is foreshadowed in the Old. The Bible is about God's saving work and self-revelation through law and prophets, Christ being the head and climax.

Scripture became the self-evident basis but because the Bible without the Church becomes a mere collection of ancient documents, Scriptural interpretation depends on the appeal to antiquity as mutually inclusive. Herein is maintained the Catholic notion of a perfect union between the Church and Scripture in that the Church's authority is not distinct from that of Scripture but rather they are one. Anglican divinity has an ecclesial context in which the Church bears witness to the truth not by reminiscence or from the words of others, but from its own living, unceasing experience, from its Catholic fullness that has its roots in the Primitive Church. This appeal is not merely to history but to a charismatic principle, tradition, which together with Scripture contains the truth of divine revelation, a truth that lives in the Church. In this spirit Anglican divines looked to the Fathers as interpreters of Scripture. *The 1571 Canons* authorise preachers to preach nothing but what is found in Holy Scripture and what the ancient Fathers have collected from the same, ensuring that the interpretation of Scripture is consistent with what Christians have believed always, everywhere and by all.

The third feature in this theological method is the appeal to reason. In creation God reveals himself as the principle of rationality, purpose and unity, described as the divine *Logos* that informs our consciences and minds enabling us to perceive purpose and order in the universe. Such knowledge requires revelation to complete it and redemption to cleanse and free the heart and mind from things that inhibit and corrupt us. It is an appeal within the context of the appeal to Scripture and antiquity. Unbalancing in one direction degenerates into the ghetto mentality of either Scripturalism or Traditionalism or Liberalism.

Today's fashionable addition of *experience* is unnecessary because tradition enfolds past and present, and embraces as its source and power the contemporaneity of the Gospel through which the true character of present experience is refracted and thereby critically evaluated. It is a way of looking at and experiencing the world; but with the kingdom of God, the *sui generis* experience of the Church and not the world as the ultimate term of reference.

Anglican Divines

This threefold appeal is found in the Reformers and in
Anglican divines following Hooker; such people as
Andrewes, Laud, Hammond, Thorndike and Taylor and
many others. An ecclesiastical use of antiquity and reason
is found in Daniel Waterland, to defend the scriptural
doctrines of the Trinity and Incarnation against Deists and
English Arians in the eighteenth century. Evangelicals like
Venn and Simeon emphasised personal experience and
commitment to Christ, but held the doctrines contained in
the Articles, Prayer Book and Homilies, as did the
Cambridge Platonists and Bishop Butler in their concern
for a reasonable faith. Evangelicals enriched the Oxford
Movement when people like Newman and others from
Evangelical homes became leading Tractarians. The nineteenth-century scientific undermining of Christianity
found this threefold appeal able to respond to and absorb
scientific method and historical criticism.

This spirit continued where the Incarnation became
central, from Westcott, Gore and the *Lux Mundi* school to
William Temple, as they illustrated the presence of the
divine *Logos* to pinpoint the unique revelation of God in
Christ as the keystone of a continuous divine activity in
creation, nature, history, culture and civilisation. The
doctrine of the One Person and Two Natures of Christ
defined by the Council of Chalcedon has had a continuous
influence. Our understanding of Eucharistic sacrifice and
sacramental presence have been enhanced, and the
doctrine of the communion of saints has been seen to be
about the living and departed as one fellowship of
common prayer and praise rather than in terms of media-
tion.

Our special character, wrote William Temple in 1930, and, as
we believe, our peculiar contribution to the Universal

Church, arises from the fact that, owing to historic circumstances, we have been enabled to combine in our one fellowship the traditional Faith and Order of the Catholic Church with that immediacy of approach to God through Christ to which the Evangelical Churches especially bear witness, and freedom of intellectual inquiry, whereby the correlation of the Christian revelation and advancing knowledge is constantly effected.[4]

Reading from the Inside

The Russian Orthodox theologian Nicholas Lossky's advice to an orthodox exploring Anglicanism is to read it 'from the inside' in the works of Anglican divines, The Book of Common Prayer and the English Hymnal, and not only in Formularies.[5] Here the living tradition of Anglicanism lies hidden rather than in statements described as corporate acts of the whole Church of England. It requires sympathetically reading the other's experience with total readiness to put one's own 'traditional' formulations in question with absolute confidence in the indestructibility of truth. The writings of the divine, the hymn, the prayer, give commentary to the formulations, a definition of certain terms lacking in them, and generally yield an impression of Anglican spirituality and doctrine.

Today's Anglican will grasp Anglicanism's spirit by suspending most of the responses and unlearning most of the habits of the modern mind that have created the great gulf between this and all preceding ages. As we do not translate Shakespeare into modern English in order to understand him, so in these divines there is no easy

---

4. Oddie, *ibid.*, p. 118.
5. Nicholas Lossky, 'An Orthodox Approach to Anglicanism', in *Sobornost*, series No. 2 (Winter 1971), p. 81.

process of changing the images. Tampering with their particular expressions will only result in losing the substance of what they are saying because as Ian Ramsey claimed, such images are *disclosure models*: specific images with a depth of meaning that develop an understanding of what is presented in several directions at once. They 'are rooted in disclosures and born in insight' and hold together two things in such a way that thought about one produces some understanding in depth of the other. Anglican divines use the language and imagery of patristic theology because the poetic vision of these Fathers could only be expressed as they, in fact, expressed it. When these divines are allowed to speak in their own language there is no substitute for reading what they say as they say it, not as mere relics of the past but as living witnesses and contemporaries with us, so that what constitutes the essential feature of these divines, their charismatic life in the Church, can continue to live in the apostolic tradition they have received.

Thomas Cranmer

5

The Book of Common Prayer

This 'Spirit of Anglicanism' or 'peculiar character,' we find embodied in the Book of Common Prayer. The principle of this English Reformation may be anti-papal but it is not anti-Catholic. Cranmer's preface to the 1549 Book makes this plain, admitting to corruptions in the Common Prayers of the Church, but seeing reform to be the restoration of the intention of the ancient Fathers as to the purpose of Divine Service as being 'for a great advancement of godliness'. At the heart of the early liturgies was the reading of the whole Bible (or the greatest part thereof), yearly. The intention behind this was that the clergy, by such continuous reading and meditation in God's word, might be stirred up to godliness themselves 'and more able to exhort others by wholesome doctrine, and to confute them that were adversaries to the Truth; and further, that the people (by daily hearing of holy Scripture read in the Church) might continually profit more and more in the knowledge of God, and be the more inflamed by the love of his true Religion'. During the medieval period 'this godly and decent Order of the ancient Fathers hath been so altered ...' With a new 'Kalendar' providing for an orderly reading of Holy Scripture and certain Rules, 'here you have an Order for Prayer, and for the reading of the Holy Scripture, much agreeable to the mind and purpose of the old Fathers.'

Evan Daniel[1] pointed out that the principles which guided the Prayer Book revisers were simple. Doctrinally they took for their standard of orthodoxy the Bible, and the belief of the Church of the first five centuries; in framing Formularies for public worship, they retained whatsoever they could of the old service books; in ritual matters they continued to follow the traditions of their own Church, deviating from them only where spiritual edification rendered such deviation necessary. Their object was not to revolutionise but to reform; not to get as far away as possible from the Church of Rome, or from any other Church, but by retracing the steps whereby the primitive Church of England had 'fallen from herself to return to Catholic faith and practice'. Hence Queen Elizabeth was perfectly justified in saying in her letter to the Roman Catholic princes, that 'there was no new faith propagated in England, no new religion set up but that which was commanded by our Saviour, practised by the primitive Church and approved by the Fathers of the best antiquity'. The same principles are distinctly and authoritatively set forth in the 30th Canon Ecclesiastical which says:

> So far was it from the purpose of the Church of England to forsake and reject the Churches of Italy, France, Spain, Germany, or any such-like Churches, in all things which they held and practised, that, as the Apology of the Church of England confesseth, it doth with reverence retain those ceremonies which do neither endamage the Church of God nor offend the minds of sober men; only departed from them in those particular points wherein they were fallen both from themselves in their ancient integrity, and from the Apostolical Churches which were their first founders.'[2]

[1.] E. Daniel, *The Prayer Book. Its History, Language and Contents* (Wells Gardner, Darton & Co., 1901), pp. 29–30.

[2.] Daniel, *ibid.*, p. 30.

Reformation not Innovation

Wheatly also points out that in revising the Liturgy of the day,

> ... it was not the design of our Reformers ... to introduce a new form of worship into the Church, but to correct and amend the old one ... and so to render the divine service more agreeable to the Scriptures, and to the doctrine and practice of the primitive Church in the best and purest ages of Christianity. Dr. Comber described the character of the Prayer Book that 'its doctrine is pure and primitive; its ceremonies so few and innocent, that most of the Christian world agree in them; ... its language ... most of the words and phrases being taken out of the Holy Scriptures, and the rest are the expression of the first and purest ages' ...[3]

In the opinion of Grotius the English Liturgy comes so near to the primitive pattern that none of the Reformed Churches can compare with it.[4] So F. D. Maurice, one of Anglicanism's greatest theologians in the nineteenth century, whose theology had its roots in St John and the Greek Fathers, could say,

> The Liturgy has been to me a great theological teacher; a perpetual testimony that the Father, the Son and the Spirit, the one God blessed for ever, is the author of all life, freedom, unity to men; that our prayers are nothing but responses to His voice speaking to us and in us.[5]

He meant that the Prayer Book is not only a manual of public devotion, but that it contains the fullest statement of the teaching of the Church. In its lections from Holy Scrip-

3. C. Wheatly, *A Rational Illustration of the Book of Common Prayer of the Church of England* (J. Bohn, 1848), Preface.
4. H. Grotius, *Ep. Ad Boet.*
5. F. D. Maurice, *Life*, vol. II, p. 359.

ture, its creeds, its prayers, its thanksgivings and exhorta-
tions, its confessions and absolutions, the occasional
offices, it brings before us the great articles of the Christian
faith in what we may call their natural order and proportion, in their organic relation to other truths, and with
constant practical reference to their subjective aspects. In
the Thirty-nine Articles these doctrines are set forth mainly
as objective truths; the Prayer Book connects them directly
with our spiritual needs and our daily conduct.

Furthermore, the Prayer Book is thoroughly Scriptural.
For Cranmer the inspiration for this general diffusion of the
Bible for 'vulgar people' in the 'vulgar tongue,' came from
his reading of the Fathers, and from the fact that the Anglo-
Saxons had translated the Bible and read it in what was
their 'vulgar tongue.' Bede is a prime example, who in the
hours before he died was busy translating St John's Gospel
into the vernacular. To this end Cranmer's liturgical revision was concerned to embody such biblical material in its
lections. It is to the Fathers he appeals to justify an English
Bible, in the face of petty quibbling objections from bishops.
In a *Prologue* or *Preface*, prefixed to the *Great Bible of 1540*, he
quoted from St John Chrysostom's sermon '*De Lazaro*,' on
the benefits 'lay and vulgar people' will derive from
reading the Scriptures. Chrysostom's concern is that those
who listen to his sermons should read their Bibles at home
between these sermons and memorise what he has
preached on such texts as they read; 'and also that they
might have their minds the more ready and better prepared
to receive and perceive that which he should say from
thenceforth in his sermons.' St Gregory Nazianzen is
quoted to reprove the idle babblers and talkers about Scripture who showed no increase of virtue or example of good
living. Anglicans can be thankful that through the influence
of the teaching of the Fathers an English Bible was authorised and their liturgy packed with biblical material that is

read and heard throughout a continuous cycle. In his preface to the first Book of Common Prayer in English Cranmer emphasised the importance of both *reading and hearing* the Scriptures following the pattern set by the early Fathers of the Church.

When one examines the Lectionary for Holy Communion in the first edition of the Book of Common Prayer of 1549, or in later editions such as that of 1662, one notices several things. First, its content is printed *in full* inside the Prayer Book; that is, the Epistle and the Gospel are there to be followed as they are read by the Priest (as is the Collect for the Day). We may presume that these readings are to be taken most seriously as they comprise nearly one third of the whole book. Secondly, the Lectionary is ancient, having existed for a millennium and having its origins in the practice and order of the Early Church. And thirdly, there is a definite, doctrinal and spiritual logic to it.

A Second Prayer Book appeared in 1552 under Protestant influences that came from within the nation and from Continental Reformers such as Martin Bucer before Queen Mary restored the Church of England to the obedience of the papacy. Elizabeth I restored the proscribed Prayer Book with minor revisions in 1559 so that it became part of the life of the nation. For Puritans and Separatists it became a symbol of Popery and came under attack but survived the Millenary to James I in 1603 and the Hampton Court Conference changes in 1604. During the Commonwealth it was suppressed and replaced by a *Directory of Worship* but was restored in 1660 with the Savoy Conference in 1661, preparing the way for revision and additions in the provision of a new Prayer Book in 1662. Since then it has been central in the continuity and development in English Church life as it has witnessed to the *faith once and for all delivered to the saints.*

The BCP has proved its worth through the history of the Church of England since its inception as a distinct branch of the Catholic Church until now. Its words have been devoutly uttered in ancient cathedrals and temporary mission churches, in the slums of great cities and the peace of little villages, in many accents and under different skies. It has expressed the faith of the simple and the learned, old and young, through the changes and frequent distresses of four and a half centuries. It has received the new baby into the fellowship of the Church, and committed the faithful Christian full of years to rest.

The BCP has shown its comprehensiveness in the movements which have so often renewed the Church of England and brought fresh emphasis to some aspect of its treasures. It was the book of the Evangelical Revival and of the Oxford Movement. It has been used with the greatest simplicity and with high ceremonial. The great Anglican divines of every shade of churchmanship, Laud, Taylor, Law, Wilberforce, Pusey, Gore, Temple and many others, have known it as their service book and drawn upon it as a vital source of their spirituality.[6]

---

6. Raymond Chapman, *A Godly and Decent Order* (Prayer Book Society Publication), p. 21.

Lancelot Andrewes

6

The Source and Context of Anglican Theology

So the theology of the Reformers and their successors must find its origin and explanation in the Book of Common Prayer. Here is a fundamental principle of patristic theology: that the corporate worship of the Church is the context of Christian thinking, the source of theology, and, as we have already noted, it kept together theology and experience, intellect and intuition, thinking and praying. Rooted in the Fathers, Anglicanism has always sought to keep these things together. The concern has always been for an ideal of theology which was not divorced from prayer and liturgy, for a way of life and worship informed and structured by theological vision. We have a patristic theology when we rediscover the Eucharist, the liturgical character of the Church's life in which we experience the Church, not as mere institution, doctrine or system but as the all-embracing *Life, Resurrection-life*, life that is salvation, because in such saving life we pass into the reality of redemption and transfiguration. The *appeal to the Fathers* in the Reformers is much more than an historical reference to the past but is an appeal to the *mind of the Fathers*, and to follow them means to acquire their mind.

The Mind of the Fathers

What do we mean by acquiring the *mind of the Fathers*? It does not mean the acquiring of an ideology, because for these men theology was far from being a mere speculative intellectual system to do with God. It is not a system of thought, but is a vision of God that is transmitted through the praying and worshipping life of the Church. What characterises these giants of Christian antiquity is the way in which in their lives they combined holiness of life, orthodoxy of doctrine and ecclesiastical approval, because they are men who primarily live 'in the depth of the Holy Spirit', continuously ascending towards the 'luminous darkness', and finally enjoying not only the writings about the Holy Trinity but living in communion with the Trinity. Therefore theology for them is not merely thinking about God but an attempt to translate into intelligible terms the experience of life in God in that central vision of Christian faith – Jesus Christ, Incarnate, Crucified, Risen and Glorified. They are not promoting anti-intellectualism, for these Fathers of the Church were knowledgeable in almost all the sciences of their times and able to use this knowledge in intellectual argumentation. But above and beyond all these human charismata we find in them a unanimous consent and agreement concerning the *true and Catholic doctrine of the Church, without any doubt or scruple*. That means that they speak from within the Church and for the Church and to acquire their *mind* is to acquire a scriptural mind and thereby come to know the mind of Christ.

It is the vision of God's creation filled with his energy and wisdom, the presence of God participating in his world which can be the only context within which to speak of man's participation in God in terms of deification. 'The Word of God, who is God, wills in all things and at all times to work the mystery of his embodiment.'[1] Within this context Hooker expounds a vision of man which finds its fulfilment in God, a theocentric humanism.

> If then in him we are blessed, it is by force of participation and conjunction with him ... so that although we be men, yet being into God united we live as it were the life of God.[2]

Lancelot Andrewes

What I am suggesting is not some esoteric dream but that which is endemic to Anglicanism, as I have already illustrated. To see it in more concrete terms, take a brief look at that truly representative Anglican, Lancelot Andrewes. In that critical sub-Reformation era he did much to determine the subsequent life and thought of the Church of England. However, as Douglas Macleane states '... it is the sweet, holy and patristic character of the man which chiefly has made his name to be reverenced among succeeding generations ... the Fathers are not more faithfully cited in his books than lively copied out in his countenance and carriage ...'[3]

True theology is always mystical, which means that it is a spirituality expressing a doctrinal attitude whose roots lie in the praying and worshipping Church. The theology of Andrewes is mystical in this sense. For him, spirituality and theology are not opposed, but the one cannot be conceived without the other. As Nicholas Lossky points out, spirituality, a modern term not used by Andrewes,

---

[1.] A. M. Allchin, *Participation in God* (DLT, 1988), p. 9, (citing Maximos the Confessor).

[2.] Hooker, *ibid.*, book I, 11, 2.

[3.] Douglas Macleane, *Lancelot Andrewes, and the Recation* (George Allen and Unwin and Sons, (1910), Preface.

means the experience in the Church of the union of man with God, and it does not mean an individualistic pietism. So for Andrewes theology is not a speculative intellectual system about God, but the translating of this ecclesial experience into terms that can be used to transmit it. It is, therefore, a vision of God, not a system of thought. This is a theology that can be preached and the aim of Andrewes's preaching is to convert his hearers to this experience of God in the rectitude of the *lex credendi* (the rule of faith) which cannot but be in profound harmony with the *lex orandi* (the rule of prayer). In consequence, Andrewes is not content merely to quote the Fathers because he has integrated in himself their essential attitude to theology itself, which is not thinking about God but the attempt to translate into intelligible terms the experience of life in God. This acquiring of the *mind of the Fathers* is what makes Andrewes himself a Father of the Church, because a Father is not confined to one age but can live in any age when there are persons who have acquired that essential attitude to theology that characterises the mind of the Fathers.

The base of that theology is summarised in his own words that we have already quoted, 'One canon reduced to writing by God himself, two testaments, three creeds, four general councils, five centuries, and the series of Fathers in that period ... determine the boundary of our faith.'[4] He is saying that the authority of the Church of England is based on the Scriptures, and on the fact that her faith is that of the Church of the first five centuries, and she holds as *of the Faith*, neither more nor less than did the Fathers. This was not antiquarianism because Andrewes does not imply that all subsequent developments are to be condemned, provided they are not held to be of the Faith,

---

4. Andrewes, *ibid.*, p. 91.

nor does he contemplate a return to the precise conditions of the Primitive Church. His concern is to provide a standard within the history of the Church, by which the development of doctrines and institutions might be tested, identifying that standard or norm of faith in its purest form in the New Testament and in the first five centuries of Church history. This continuity of Anglicanism with antiquity meant that the Anglican Church was part of the One Holy Catholic and Apostolic Church. The *primitivism* of Andrewes is by no means a simple return to the past nor can it be ever a search for some 'golden age' as a period of reference *par excellence*. The 'tradition' of the Church can never be reduced to a simple conservation of what has been said or done in the past.

> It is a dynamic process that transcends linear time, without in any way abolishing it. It is, in fact, a way of living in time in the light of eternity, which recapitulates past, present, and future because everything is lived in contemporaneity with the reality of the Gospel. What the Churches of God have done at all times is of importance to Andrewes, not in a spirit of imitation or conservatism, but to the extent that they have done it in a consciousness of living by 'memorial', 'anamnesis', the past events of the Gospel and their consequences to come, in the Church of the present.[5]

Dean Church pointed out that Andrewes recalled an age that otherwise would have been stifled in the looms of Protestant scholasticism, into a diviner, purer, freer air, back to the many-sided thought, to the sanctified divinity of the undivided Church. By the influence of this divinity he led his contemporaries away from a theology which ended in cross-grained and perverse conscientiousness to

---

5. N. Lossky, *Lancelot Andrewes the Preacher (1555–1626): The Origins of the Mystical Theology of the Church of England*, trans. Andrew Louth (Clarendon Press, 1991), p. 340.

a theology which ended in adoration, self-surrender and blessing, and in the awe and joy of welcoming the Eternal Beauty, the Eternal Sanctity and the Eternal Love, the Sacrifice and Reconciliation of the world.[6] This fusion of thought and feeling in Hooker and Andrewes is what drew that twentieth-century man of letters, T. S. Eliot, back to Christian faith and life and prompted his small book of essays *For Lancelot Andrewes*, who for Eliot embodied in himself the learning, the theology and the devotion which marks the best men of this age. For Eliot, Hooker and Andrewes made the English Church more worthy of intellectual assent, and in them, as in the actual life and worship of the period, he found a Catholicism which was not ignorant either of the Renaissance or the Reformation. Here for Eliot was a tradition which had already moved into the modern world, which was a way of living and thinking the Christian tradition and which had taken humanism and criticism into itself, without being destroyed by them.

Throughout the centuries this tradition has, in addition to C. S. Lewis and T. S. Eliot, inspired other creative writers. Here are a number of representative names that is by no means an exhaustive list. John Donne (1571–1631) the famous Dean of St Paul's, a metaphysical poet, preacher and convert from Roman Catholicism encouraged George Herbert (1593–1633), the poet, priest and pastor who influenced other poets such as T. S. Eliot. Herbert's poetry is representative of the Anglican Communion, his great book being *The Temple*. His writing is the fruit of an integrated life in which the vocation of poet, priest and pastor is richly blended. It is why he lives and continues to speak to every age bringing that touch of

---

6. R. Church, 'Lancelot Andrewes', in *Masters of English Theology*, ed. A. Barry (London, 1877), p. 90.

heaven into the ordinary. Herbert was the father of poets. Henry Vaughan, another seventeenth-century poet, a convert from earthly to divine love, was a spiritual son of Herbert, a diligent and excellent churchman who deplored the religious disharmony of his time, and whose desire was not so much for order in conduct as for unity in the soul.[7] This sensitivity to see the extraordinary in the ordinary is present in the poetry of Thomas Traherne (1637–1674), like Herbert a priest and poet, whose works were accidentally discovered early in the twentieth century. Traherne's poetry speaks of prayer and the vision that is born of it, the vision of a transfigured world which is seen in *The Way of a Pilgrim* and is at the heart of Eastern Orthodoxy but also is present in our own tradition. This devotional poetry emerges from an active state of mind and spirit sensitive to the presence of God that is seeking union with him in words. Thomas Ken (1637–1711), the non-juring bishop, is well known for his two famous morning and evening hymns, *Awake, My Soul, and with the Sun* and *Glory to Thee My God, this Night* and his *Manual of Prayers.*

In the eighteenth century we have the evangelical piety of Henry Venn (1725–1797) in his prose work *The Complete Duty of Man,* the hymns and poems of John and Charles Wesley, and Harriet Auber (1773–1862), the author of many devotional poems, of *The Spirit of the Psalms* (1829) and the well-known hymn *Our Blest Redeemer, ere He breathed.* The Hymnal is a manual of doctrine and devotion, a treasury of creative devotional poetry from which the laity learn their theology. It is in the nineteenth century that we find another book in which the poetry of the Anglican Communion is happily represented: John

---

[7] Edward Dowden, *Puritan and Anglican: Studies in Literature* (Kegan Paul, Trench, Trübner & Co. Ltd., 1910), p. 121.

Keble's *The Christian Year*. This collection is designed to exhibit 'the soothing tendency of the Prayer Book'. He uses the word 'soothng' that comes from finding the 'peace of God which passes all understanding'. The 'soothing' grace which Christ brings is the healing, strengthening and ordering power of the Spirit that is at the heart of Christian worship. Hence, Keble's sense that the Prayer Book has a 'soothing tendency.' In Keble's poetry we see the influence of that rediscovery of the symbolic, sacramental and imaginative character of the Christian Revelation.

> Both the poet and the man of faith are called to a whole-hearted commitment and attentiveness. And so Keble warns that 'no poet will ever be great who does not constantly spend time and toil in studying the beauty of earth and sky so as to make every detail of the whole bear upon the object of his own love and enthusiasm'. No more 'will any one make the slightest progress in holiness and piety who is content with the empty praises of good books or good men and makes no attempt to imitate them in his own life'. From the poetry of the heart fostered by such discipline Keble looked to see a re-kindling of the Christian imagination, and he himself notably contributed to it.[8]

In that same period is Christina Rossetti (1830–1894), a devout member of the Church of England and one of England's foremost women poets, whose poetry and prose is characterised by spiritual, longing. Charlotte Yonge (1823–1901) was prepared for confirmation by John Keble and was described as 'the spiritual child of Mr Keble, whose novels and stories reached a wide public and won her a secure place in English literature'.[9] She is securely

---

8. Geoffrey Rowell, *The Vision: GloriousThemes and Personalities of the Catholic Revival in Anglicanism* (OUP, 1983), p. 33.
9. S. L. Ollard, *A Short History of the Oxford Movement* (Mowbrays, 1915), p. 220.

placed as a loyal member of the Church of England and her books could be given out by parents to their children in the certainty that they would improve their minds. She became a teacher and was the author of many fiction and non-fiction works, including her best-seller, *The Heir of Redclyffe* (1853).

> Mr. Keble was always her intimate friend and guide ... Her writings have influenced at least two generations. She made the idea of the Church as a great living force really a working principle in the lives of many of her readers. Throughout her quiet, almost uneventful, life she worked incessantly for the glory of God and the good of His Church. She showed in every book how intimately creed and character are intertwined; she tried to inculcate always, not by direct words but by implication, that the one thing needful 'is to find out what God requires me to do' ... She exalted the domestic virtues, and invested 'the trivial round, the common task' with an atmosphere of romance; and she had a passion for goodness, and a desire that people should use their circumstances as opportunities for the development and training of character. But she never lost sight of the possibility of calls to other than the purely domestic career. She became in 1868 an Exterior Sister of the Community of St Mary the Virgin Wantage.[10]

As her spiritual mentor, John Keble was a great influence on Yonge's fiction and educational writings as an exponent on morality. She popularised the ideals of the Oxford Movement that she had embraced, devoting her life to teaching children, assisting in church building, and supporting foreign missions. Her influence on the women educators of her day and generations to come was profound.

---

10. G. J. Romanes, *Dictionary of English Church History*, ed. Ollard and Crosse (A. R. Mowbray, 1912), p. 661.

The twentieth-century has, alongside T. S. Eliot and C. S. Lewis, the poetry and prose of John Betjeman, the poetry of R. S. Thomas, the outstanding poet of the latter part of the century, and the prose works of Dorothy L. Sayers and Evelyn Underhill.

A Church that could nurture and satisfy such people with their humility, their wisdom, their learning and overflowing love, the strength and capacity of their conviction and unceasing devotion to God, is a Church in which the depth and richness of religious experience can be known. The final goal of all theology is union with God and in this sense theology is always mystical and is not a question of an exceptional experience reserved for a few. It is a question of the interiorisation of the revealed Christian mystery, to which Andrewes calls all the baptised. This theology is mystical in the sense that it is not an abstract reflection, but a concrete way of living the mystery in the deepening of the faith through prayer and the renunciation of one's own will. It is a way of the submission of the human to the divine will, which allows the Holy Spirit to impregnate human nature. For Andrewes this is only possible in fidelity to the given realities of revelation, that is to say, in the scriptural and patristic tradition or in other words in the Catholicity of the Church.

> Keble protested against many of the academic theologians of his day for their 'habit of resolving the high mysteries of the faith into mere circumstances of language, methods of speaking adapted to our weak understanding, but with no real counterpart in the nature of things.' We must be alert, he says, to the danger of 'slighting divine mysteries because we cannot comprehend and explain them,' and he is never tired of reminding his hearers that it is only the pure in heart who see God. Theology is properly doxology, worship, and so there must always be a sense of awe and wonder in our approach to God, whether as theologians or as Christian believers. Theology and spirituality must be closely joined.

Keble's theology, like that of the Orthodox churches both today and throughout their history, can be properly said to be mystical theology, prayed theology.[11]

11. Rowell, *ibid.*, p. 34.

Charles I on his way to execution.

On 30th January 1649 King Charles accompanied by William Juxon, Bishop of London, walked through St James's Park to Whitehall where the scaffold awaited.

7

During the Interregnum

When the Church of England was suffering persecution in the time of Cromwell, it was to Dr Hammond, more than to any other single man, that she owed the continuance of her existence ... It was by his holiness, charity and devoted labours that a tone was given to the clergy of that period which bore good fruit afterwards.[1]

The Interregnum was the time between 1649, the year of Charles I's execution by a parliament dominated by Puritans, and the restoration in 1660–62 of the Church of England and the Book of Common Prayer. During this time Henry Hammond was the embodiment of Anglicanism when Cromwell attempted to make the Church of England Puritan and a Puritan Parliament forbade the use of the Book of Common Prayer replacing it with *A Directory of Worship*. Attempts were made to destroy the identity of the Church of England and in consequence the Anglican mind.

Henry Hammond (1605–1660) was in the tradition of Hooker and Andrewes, expressing himself in the same kind of way and through his writings illustrating the impact of the *Ecclesiastical Polity* in the thought of the day. It is not surprising to find that a balanced relationship between Scripture, antiquity and reason formed the core of his theological method. There is a resemblance to

---

[1.] G. G. Perry, *Life of Henry Hammond* (SPCK, n.d.), p. 3.

Andrewes, not in the style of his general approach but in interests, both finding a common concern for antiquity and history, biblical texts and language, liturgical and devotional matters. Grotius, the Dutch scholar, shared the basic conviction of Hammond's ecclesiology that the Church of England was 'the most careful observer, and transcriber of primitive antiquity'. William Teale writes:

> the present is a time when it is desirable to remind many that men whose excellence is admitted by persons holding opposite theological sentiments, were not less remarkable for orthodoxy than sanctity; that they were zealous observers of all the means of grace, strict disciplinarians, and unflinching maintainers of doctrines and practices, which by not a few are considered to be incompatible with genuine piety. On the other hand, it will be satisfactory, to those whose minds may have been unsettled by recent controversies, to observe how the highest reverence for the Church universal may coexist with dutiful allegiance to the Church of England.
>
> Nor is the writer without hope that the account which he has given of the writings of these famous doctors may be found useful to students in theology and to the younger clergy, by directing their attention to works which are at once the honour of our literature and treasures of Christian truth,—which present a fair portraiture of the doctrine and discipline of the English Church, and may be followed as safe guides in either. [2]

Such men as Hammond were fully aware that

> the Church could not survive its days of adversity by a policy of mere aloofness and obstruction, but must justify its intransigence on theological and historical grounds. It is due in large measure to his efforts and his encouragement of others that the Interregnum became in fact a golden age of High Anglican theology and apologetic.[3]

[2.] William Teale, *Lives of English Divines* (Masters, 1846), pp. vi–vii.
[3.] R. S. Bosher, *The Making of the Restoration Settlement* (Dacre Press, 1951), p. 36.

Hammond was the first to realise that a defence of Anglicanism must be intellectually sound. His aim and that of his circle was to build an edifice of reasoned theology in support of Laudian Church principles, which not only moderated them but made them intelligible to their opponents.

This need was crucially urgent so Hammond began building an intellectual defence for the faith, whose outward structure, the Church, lay in ruins. It was a banned and persecuted Church that was forbidden to use the Book of Common Prayer, celebrate Christmas, Easter or Whitsun and in the parishes Anglican priests were replaced by Presbyterian ministers and bishops abolished. Despite this antipathy towards, and persecution of, everything the Church of England stood for, Hammond's dream was slowly being realised as the theological output at this time became an impressive witness to the strength of Anglican orthodoxy in a young school of theologians nurtured by William Laud before his execution. There appeared such classics as Pearson's *Exposition of the Creed*, Thorndike's *Epilogue to the Tragedy of the Church of England*, Taylor's *The Real Presence* and *Ductor Dubitaniium*, and Sparrow's *Rationale upon the Book of Common Prayer*.

Alongside this solid array of learning, there appeared a host of popular controversial works, now forgotten, but effective propaganda in their day. All championed Anglican orthodoxy in the tradition of Hooker, Andrewes and Laud. This became the Laudian viewpoint in popular treatises. The effect of these publications on public opinion is hard to estimate, but one result may be seen in the steady demand for Episcopal ordination. In a day when the pulpit was a public platform and theological debate a public entertainment, the Laudians did not hesitate to make use of 'disputations' to broadcast their views.

Another way of propagating their views was to encourage the introduction of orthodox divines into the homes of the nobility and gentry as tutors and chaplains. Such dispossessed clergy in a proscribed and persecuted Church were able to encourage a generation of young English squires to absorb the principles of Anglican orthodoxy so that this alliance of Squire and Laudian became an influence in politics for the next hundred years. Here in these houses the services of the Prayer Book were celebrated with new devotion so that by the mid-1650s orthodox Anglicans assumed an importance that could not have been predicted a decade earlier. It led to the victory of Laudians over Puritans and Presbyterians that produced the 1662 Book of Common Prayer and the restoration not only of the Church of England but also of the Anglican mind.

Hammond venerated Ignatius of Antioch as a defender of episcopacy. Ignatius's letters during his journey to Rome expounded the meaning of episcopacy as God's gift to the Church, ensuring God's grace through the Sacraments and our salvation. He wrote letters to Rome pleading with the Christians not to try and save him from martyrdom, which he saw as necessary if episcopacy was to survive in the Church. When episcopacy was threatened by Cromwell and the Puritans in the Church of England, it was Hammond who rediscovered that Ignatius regarded episcopacy as the best safeguard of the unity of the Church, and that without the bishop's authority the Eucharist could not be celebrated. If it could be proved that the authority of Ignatius's support for episcopacy was genuine, a severe blow would be dealt to those opposed to bishops. Hammond published *Of The Power of the Keyes; or Of Binding and Loosing,* in which he examined the evidence of Scripture and the Fathers concerning the nature of church government. There is a detailed examination of the support given by the Fathers to the Order of Bishops, and a special appeal to the Ignatian letters.

Also, Hammond venerated Vincent of Lérins for his credal canon; this showed where orthodox teaching is to be found. It is summed up in the phrase that 'we believe, what has been believed everywhere, always and by everyone'. Again, Hammond was convinced that an important place must be given to the liturgy in the guardianship of apostolic faith; it was 'a hedge to keep out errors'. Hence, Hammond has been described as 'Learned in School-divinity, and a master in Church-antiquity, perfect and ready in the sense of the Fathers, Councils, ecclesiastical historians and liturgies'.[4] Hammond was a key theologian for Keble, as later for Newman.

Professor Owen Chadwick wrote:

… if High Churchmen of that age like Bramhall or Thorndike had been asked what led them not to compromise, they would have replied in terms like the following:

Our paramount duty is to the Catholic Church; our subordinate and derivative duty is to the Church of England as the representative of the Catholic Church in this country. The Catholic Church is known by its faithfulness to the primitive model. The Church of England has no choice but to follow that model, must seek to apply the principle rigorously and exactly. 'I am satisfied,' wrote Thorndike in 1660, 'that the differences, upon which we are divided, cannot be justly settled upon any terms, which any part of the *Whole* Church shall have just cause to refuse, as inconsistent with the unity of the *Whole* Church.' He has an ominous phrase about men 'ordained by Presbyters against Bishops' – how shall we recognize as ordained, men who were ordained for the purpose of setting up altar against altar? The Church of England is to be re-established by law; and if some pretend tenderness of conscience against that law, some might pretend tenderness of conscience against any law. As Thorndike wrote in *Just Weights and Measures*: 'Supposing the Unity of

---

4. John Fell's *Life of Hammond* (appended to This works in the Library of Anglo-Catholic Theology).

the Church ordained by God; to forbear those Laws which it requireth, because tenderness of conscience may be alleged against them, is to offend the whole rather than a part. For the same might have been alleged against any Law of God's Church.'

The argument ... represents a contention which has survived the centuries and must still be reckoned with. Any act which divides the Church of England from the universal Church of the centuries is to be eschewed, even if that act offers temporary or local advantage; and the test of universality, in this sad, divided state of Christendom, may be found in appeal to the ancient and undivided Church of the first centuries. The question whether there are sufficient ambiguities or exceptions in the Episcopal practice of the ancient Church to warrant modern exceptions, Thorndike answered with a vigorous negative. The question whether these objections against an act in breach of Catholicity apply with equal force to a temporary, an interim, exception to episcopacy as a charitable remedy for an anomalous predicament, he made no attempt to consider.[5]

5. Geoffrey F. Nuttall and Owen Chadwick (eds), *From Uniformity to Unity, 1662–1962* (SPCK, 1962), pp. 13ff (original emphasis).

John Keble

8

The Spirit of Tractarianism

In the nineteenth century we find in John Keble and the leaders of the Oxford Movement people rooted deeply in continuity with the past and who possessed a strong sense of the sanctity of order and tradition. To them the shallow and self-confident rationalism of liberalism was supremely distasteful. Keble's father had introduced him to the wide-mindedness and sanctified divinity of the great Anglican divines of the seventeenth century with its roots in the early Fathers of the Church. Richard Hooker, the author of the *Laws of Ecclesiastical Polity*, was a former student of his college, Corpus Christi; and in 1835 Keble edited the *Works* of Hooker. It would seem that Hooker's 'resolution to make the best of things as they were, and to censure as rarely and as tenderly as possible what he found established by authority', affected him and deepened the tendencies of Keble's own character. From Hooker he learned that episcopal authority rested on divine appointment, yet the acute situation of his time compelled him to make qualifications. This was seen to be impossible after the fuller vindication of episcopacy in the Ignatian epistles by Archbishop Ussher. Keble wrote to Froude – 'I am more and more satisfied that Richard was in most things a middle term between Laud and Cranmer, but nearer the former; and also that he was in a transition state when he was taken from us, and there is no saying how much nearer he might have got to Laud, if he had lived twenty years longer.'

Yet with all these limitations, Hooker – with his reverent treatment of the deepest doctrines, his faith in the reality of Sacramental grace, his sense of the quasisacramental value of all Church usages, his treatment of fast and festival and of Church property as all being expressions of man's sacrifice to God – seemed to Keble God's chief instrument for saving the Church from rationalism in the sixteenth century. Keble's concern was for the perils present in the nineteenth-century Church of England. His hope was that these volumes of Hooker might be instrumental in awakening the Church of England in the nineteenth century to a sense of that danger, by focusing their attention on the primitive Apostolic Church and its faith and order as the ark of refuge divinely appointed for the faithful.

Henry Hammond's Influence

Another influential Anglican divine, from Laud's time, was Henry Hammond, who by his holiness, charity and devoted labours had impressed a tone upon the clergy of that period which bore good fruit afterwards. As we have seen he is the embodiment of Anglicanism in the seventeenth century in the tradition of Hooker, Andrewes and Laud, expressing himself in the same kind of way and through his writings illustrating the impact of the *Ecclesiastical Polity* in the thought of the day. It was such seventeenth-century theologians as these that moulded the character of Keble's father as a priest and through his father's influence, Keble himself. This was no mere conservatism or abstract tradition but *the* living tradition – the continuity on English soil of the Primitive Church in its apostolic faith and order that anchors it in the original events of the Gospels. It must be emphasised again, this is the *tradition of truth* in which is the apostolic teaching. This apostolic teaching is not so much an unchangeable example to be repeated or imitated; it is an eternally living and inexhaustible source of life and inspiration. Tradition is the constant abiding Spirit, not only the memory of words, and is therefore a charismatic, not an historical principle. Together with Scripture it contains the truth of divine revelation, a truth that lives in the Church. Then theology becomes not primarily a matter of intellectual clarity, but the union of human lives with God in the way of holiness. This is saving life, salvation-life. Thus Keble's poem:

> *Blest are the pure in heart,*
> *For they shall see our God,*
> *The secret of the Lord is theirs,*
> *Their soul is Christ's abode.*

In other words, the climax of purity is the threshold of theology.

Is it no wonder that Keble was outraged at the action of the government in their interference in the affairs of the Church in abolishing six Irish bishoprics? His objection was theological, not political. Bishops were a divine institution, God's gift to his Church, and not man-made. Man could not tamper with God's gifts. Episcopacy was the guarantor of the sacramental order of the Church and to tamper with it is to risk losing the means of our salvation, the saving life.

The Tractarian Influence

In an article entitled 'National Apostasy Now',[1] the late Canon Professor Roy Porter recalls the question asked by the Tractarians: Why was the Church so weak in the face of the dangers which threatened it? They concluded that 'the dangers were not simply from the outside but were also there in the actual life of the Church of their day.' In the words of William Palmer, 'We felt ourselves assailed by enemies from without and foes within ... enemies within the Church seeking the subversion of its essential characteristics and what was worst of all, *no principle in the public mind to which we could appeal.*' Palmer was alluding to the influence of Thomas Arnold and those associated with his latitudinarian views and for whom the Church was no more than the brotherhood of all those who professed the name of Christ. For them it was no more than an association for the promotion of religion and social virtue and matters of dogmatic belief, ecclesiastical organisation and liturgical observance were only of secondary importance. 'It was because of the widespread, if no doubt often unconscious, acceptance of such ideas that the Church lacked that clear principle by which it could define its true character and defend it against the world. Hence national apostasy and ecclesiastical apostasy were only two sides of the same coin.'

Porter points out that the same question that concerned the Oxford Fathers concerns us today: Does the Church have a distinctive and independent witness to the society in which it is set or is it to be 'conformed to this world' or is its purpose to be very much more?

[1.] All quotations in this chapter are taken from J. R. Porter, 'National Apostasy Now', in *Tracts for our Times, 1833–1983* (St Mary Bourne Street, 1983).

When we look at the bench of bishops and at so many other leading clergymen today, we may well gain the impression that they are every bit as much part of the Establishment as were their predecessors at the end of the 18th century – that is, their pronouncements and actions generally reflect a vague liberal consensus, a somewhat desperate chasing after trendiness and a feeling that change is good for its own sake, a wishy-washy ecumenism, a sentimentality and anti-intellectualism which is not only merely ignorant of theology but actually rejects it, all of which remind us very forcibly of the strictures levelled against the religious temper of the age by the fathers of the Oxford Movement.

There is an insidious worldliness in today's Church, an apostasy as real as that which Keble preached against in his day. Today it intrudes itself as political correctness that is tearing the Anglican Communion apart in the struggle of two incompatible religions. What we miss in our bishops, claims Professor Porter, is the exemplification in their teaching and work of their status and function as the apostolic ministry in and to the Church founded by Christ – and the men of the Oxford Movement missed it too. They sought to recover it by their emphasis on the apostolic succession of the episcopate. They wanted to revive an awareness of the true character of the bishop, and of the fact that that character was the most important thing about him, as the symbol of the divine origin of the whole Church and as a man possessing above all, in the words of the Lambeth Quadrilateral, 'the commission of Christ and the authority of the whole body'.

It is difficult to deny that such an understanding of the Episcopal office is not very evident in the contemporary Church of England and this is why there is so much confusion over it, not least among bishops themselves, and why it is often so difficult to get across its absolute centrality for the Church in reunion discussions. As a result, although bishops have happily ceased, or largely so, to be the State bureaucrats they once were, we have made them more than ever into ecclesiastical bureaucrats. What stands in the way of that reappraisal of the episcopal order, which is so widely felt in our Church to be necessary, is again a want of principle, a principle by which we can assess and reform: the Oxford Movement points us to where we should look for it.

But the Tractarians were also concerned with the renewal of the priesthood, by their emphasis on sacramental and priestly ideals which changed the whole character of priestly ministry and awakened the parochial clergy with their watch-cry, 'Stir up the gift that is in you.'

> What the clergy still need is a true and profound understanding of their calling to receive a 'divine commission' and then that this understanding should permeate and inform the whole of their spiritual lives. Only from this can genuine and effective priestly action flow and only then will society learn that it needs this distinctive ministry which it can find nowhere else. Catholic Renewal in our church must begin, as did the Oxford Movement, though not of course end, with the renewal of the clergy and its motto should be: 'let priests be priests.'

The Tractarians were much concerned for a return to the prescriptive sources of Anglicanism in the Fathers and the Caroline divines, not only for the renewal of the Church but also for the intellectual and spiritual formation and nourishment of the clergy. They wished to ensure that their life and work should be grounded in sound doctrine, by which they meant the traditional and orthodox faith of the Church, resting on the three pillars of the Bible, the early Fathers, the Book of Common Prayer and the Anglican divines of the seventeenth century. They saw that this was the only way in which the priestly calling and commission which we have just discussed could be realised and continued in daily life and that such studies must form the bulwark to protect the Church's faith from those foes within and without: the liberals who would water it down and conform it to a secular society's values. To this end they published the *Library of the Fathers of the Holy Catholic Church*, a series of scholarly translations of their works, and the *Library of Anglo-Catholic Theology*, editions of the works of Anglican divines. With the increased resources for study available today how many clergy know the Fathers, or anything in their own classical Anglican tradition which are crucial resources for their intellectual and devotional life? How much is today's ordinand informed of these resources in theological college? The evidence suggests that emphasis is more heavily weighted on the agenda of politically correct issues than classical Anglican theology. As Professor Porter says,

> ... can we be happy that the Church of England and its leaders apparently do so little by way of presenting a vigorous and reasoned defence of those doctrines to which they are pledged to adhere? Matters are probably even less satisfactory with regard to the knowledge by both clergy and laity of the spiritual treasures of the Anglican divines who preserved the Catholic heritage of the Church of England and whose heirs the Tractarians recognized themselves to be. Once more, Catholic Renewal must have its theological side; a re-statement and affirmation of the Church's historic faith in the circumstances of the twenty-first century, as the Oxford Movement did in the early nineteenth. But there is all too little sign of this as yet.

The classical Anglican divines and the Oxford Fathers have much to say to us of the whole tenor and temper of modern church life, for they saw the Christian life in terms of holiness, the sanctity of the individual member and the whole body of the faithful. Theology is not just a matter of intellectual clarity but the union of human lives with God in the way of holiness. So the Christian life is 'one of constant discipline where we are immersed in holy things which are to be handled in a spirit of sobriety, austerity and awe'. This is such a contrast to the loss of dignity in the casualness, laid-back 'mateyness' of much Christian worship today. For the Tractarians the Church is a supernatural body that reflects the divine holiness and this present life is a preparation for the life to come, not merely in the future but as a present eternal state that is penetrated by the 'life of the world to come'. It is this dimension of the 'life of the world to come' in our present experience that enables us to take the irksomeness of life, the conflicts and burdens, joys and sorrows, successes and failures, so that they can be transfigured with us. Our frustrations and disappointments, sufferings and conflicts, the 'thorns in the flesh,' have to be taken into that supernatural milieu. When that is done we shall find that it makes all the difference to the way in which we live through them and even look at them. They do not magically disappear; the memory of them continues and the pain may continue to hurt. But in that environment of divine life and love in which the Father lives with Jesus our crucified and glorious Lord, in the Holy Spirit, they will be transfigured. It is in this presence of the 'life of the world to come' that our social and political engagement with the world must reach out and where 'in the world' but 'not of the world,' we remind people that this eternal world is their ultimate destiny.

Michael Ramsey

9

Returning to
Prescriptive Sources

As Gareth Bennett told us, there has been a deliberate
rejection of the balanced synthesis, a balanced relationship
between Scripture, antiquity and reason that formed the
core of Anglican theological method. It is the distancing of
the modern Church from what had been regarded as its
prescriptive sources and the rejection of 'living in a tradition,' that has produced the crisis in modern Anglicanism.
In consequence we have lost the Anglican mind as God
and His Church become imprisoned within the relativism
of the present and accommodated to the transitoriness of
today's political correctness, the product of secular
humanism that is allowed to be the re-interpreter of the
Bible and the 'faith once and for all delivered to the saints'.
Only a return to prescriptive sources in the *mind of the
Fathers*, in Reformer, Caroline and Oxford Father, will lift
us into a larger room and raise us, like Hooker, Andrewes,
Hammond and our benefactors in the Oxford Movement,
above the controversies and theological fashions of our
age. Here in the larger room of the Christian centuries in
which the Holy Catholic Church lives, we will find what
will enrich, invigorate, and give beauty, proportion and
force to our theology. Our vision will have about it the
Catholicity, the wide-mindedness, the freshness, the
suppleness and sanity of Christian antiquity, as we see the

Christian faith as an integral whole with its natural centre in the Incarnation, the Church as an organism where dogma, prayer and life are one whole, and where as Michael Ramsey kept pointing out, '... the issue is not only one of intellectual clarity but of a union of human lives with God in the way of holiness'. Renewal in Catholic truth will only come from a reconstruction of the *One Holy Catholic and Apostolic Church,* not through the construction of some external religious or cultural form, or ideology. It can come only when the living pattern of Catholic truth is embodied in people imbued with the life-giving power of God, who in Christ has taken our human nature, redeemed it and perfected it for ever. The *lex credendi,* tradition, Catholic dogma and doctrine are not a backcloth of abstract theory to be adapted to the fashions of the age. This is the *reality* in which we live, *the union of human lives with God in the way of holiness.* Through it we see refracted the meaning of all human existence, the economies of creation and redemption, and hence the need to know this truth in the personal depth of our being, for it is the Christ of the Apostles as the life-giving Spirit active in the history of humankind and leading it to conformity with his spiritual and perfect form. Here in the Mystery of Christ, present in the history of mankind and the Eucharist, is where Catholic truth is found, so that our proper life-situation is *the life of grace* in which we as Catholic persons need to grow and develop to the full potential of our humanity. Salvation then becomes, not the return journey of the individual soul to its maker, but the Catholic process, the gradual process of a universal transfiguration in which people are saved, not from the world, but with the world through the Church. It is walking in the way of holiness as we live in and serve the Catholicity of the Church.

That is why we need to let these Fathers speak again:

Ignatius, Irenaeus, Athanasius, Basil, Gregory Nazianzus, Gregory of Nyssa, Ambrose and Augustine, Anselm and Aquinas, the Reformers, Jewel and Hooker, Andrewes and Laud, John Keble, the Tractarians, and Michael Ramsey. They can speak to us today with that same sharpness and contemporaneity, for their writings are timeless, dynamic and always contemporary. Let us invite the piety and thought of these Fathers into the structure of our own theological vision and exposition by emulating these benefactors in the Faith, whose theological procedure could not be described as simplistic; and let us see what happens in the different perspective of today's society and scholarship. Michael Ramsey said that the times call urgently for the Anglican witness to Scripture, tradition and reason, not only for meeting the problems Biblical theology is creating, but also to serve the reintegration of the Church in East and West and for presenting the faith as at once supernatural and related to contemporary man.

The Fathers will speak to an issue facing us that is far bigger than the saving of the Church of England. In the face of an arbitrary liberalism that supplants the true liberality that is a generosity of spirit, and a facile comprehensiveness that too often lacks a theological coherence and discernment, what we are being called upon to save is the Apostolic Faith and Order of the Church, for which Ignatius died. This Apostolic Faith and Order will challenge the uncritical assumptions of much contemporary ecumenism and not be instantly popular because it is about principles not policies, but in its appeal to Scripture and antiquity it will face it with something deeper. At the same lime it will show us how theology can, and cannot, be influenced by the culture of the age. In other parts of the world there are other Christians in the face of this same liberalism in their own churches who share our concern. Is God leading us into a new kind of unity with such Christians, a faithful remnant in which the world will see what it wants to see, a re-integrated and holy Church, reflecting the oneness and unity of the Blessed Trinity, because it is rooted in the Apostolic Faith and Order? Here lies the authentic note of a Western Orthodoxy, Catholic Christianity, for the content and significance of the Christian experience enshrined in this Apostolic Faith and Order transcends all individual apprehensions and defies all final intellectual analysis. Its authority lies in its influence on the world of an insight more adequate than the world's own. It comes in all its saving power to identify with the world but as soon as the world attempts to accommodate and trim that Apostolic Faith and Order to its own limited insights, it is lost and the world ends up shipwrecked and the Church dysfuntional. The Fathers in every age have known this: that the only way of salvation for a shipwrecked world is to be conformed to the Eucharistic self-giving of God. Let this be our ministry of reconciliation, the way for people of the tradition today whose search for truth is within this living tradition and anything that is in plain contradiction to it we cannot accept.

Appendix 1
The Rule of Faith

This Rule of Faith is described in the earliest writings that mention it as a traditional 'body of doctrine, descending from the Apostles, and even from the Lord Himself, the "faith delivered to the saints"'. Thus Irenaeus says, 'The Church, scattered though it be throughout the whole world to the very extremities thereof, hath received from the Apostles and their disciples faith in one God.'[1] Then follow the several terms of the Creed, but as scattered portions, the Church as yet being careful not to expose her sacred symbol in its integrity to the gaze and imitation of heresy. 'The Church,' he adds, 'having received this body of doctrine, in its entirety carefully guards it, as dwelling in one house; her faith is in accordance with it, and her preaching and instruction and tradition are in harmony with it, as though they were uttered with one mouth.' This form, he says elsewhere, was committed to memory.

> To which prescription those many barbarous nations assent who believe in Christ, having the saving doctrine, 'salutem', written on their hearts by the Spirit, not on parchment with ink; and diligently guarding the ancient tradition, they believe 'in one God maker of heaven and earth', &c.; the

[1] Irenaeus, *ibid.*, book I, ch. ii.

rudest nations being thereby preserved from the blasphe-
mous ravings of heresy.[2]

Similarly, Tertullian writes:

> Let us inquire then in our own body, and from our own
> record, and only so far as any question may arise, without
> prejudice to the rule of faith ... is one only God, and no other
> Creator of the world; and he gives the several clauses of the
> Creed in their true order, though amplified by a brief running
> commentary, as they have a bearing on the heresies with
> which he is dealing. This rule ... instituted, as will be shown,
> by Christ, admits of no question amongst ourselves, except
> such as are forced upon us by heresy... To know nothing in
> opposition to this rule is to know everything.[3]

Elsewhere he says, 'The rule of faith is altogether one, it
alone is invariable and unalterable, *immobilis et irreforma-
bilis* namely of faith in one God, Creator of the world &c.'[4]
And in chapter two of his treatise against Praxeas, after
running through the several clauses of the creed, he
declares 'that it descended from the beginning of the
Gospel'. Similarly Origen, after opening the subject of his
work on the principal doctrines of Christianity, gives a
running commentary on the articles of the creed. Having
judged it necessary to set out the 'unwavering line and
sure rule', he continues,

> ... let the preaching of the Church, delivered by the Apostles
> in orderly succession and abiding in the Churches to the
> present day, be maintained, which in no point differs from
> the ecclesiastical and apostolical tradition ... Now these are
> the special points that have been clearly handed down by the
> Apostolical preaching ...[5]

2. *Ibid.*, book III, ch. iv.1.
3. Tertullian, *Prescription Against Heresy*, 12, 13, 14.
4. Tertullian, *OnVirginity*, i.
5. *De Principiis.*

Then, as in other instances, follows a commentary on the various articles of the Creed.

In December 1832 Newman set off on a Mediterranean cruise with Hurrell Froude and his father. He had written poetry before and now found the leisure to write some poems. His purpose was more than the expression of a poetic instinct. The object was to assert truths with a freedom and clearness for his conviction was that stirring lines bring out poets and he hoped by this poetry to encourage others to express themselves and to create 'a quasi-political engine.' With Newman's 109 poems and Keble's forty-six the *Lyra Apostolica* was published. Newman believed that ideas become impressive when put into metrical shape. The book was used by many as a devotional manual and in the introduction to the 1901 edition was described as 'the song book of English Catholicity in its most militant and defiant mood'. The following poem, *The Rule of Faith*, expresses the fundamental premise of Tractarian theology as derived from the Primitive Church.

1
TRUTH through the Sacred Volume hidden lies,
And spreads from end to end her secret wing,
Through ritual, type, and storied mysteries.
From this or that, when Error points her sting,
From all her holds Truth's stern defences spring,
And Text to Text the full accordance bears.
Through every page the Universal King,
From Eden's loss unto the end of years,
From East unto the West, the Son of Man appears.

2

Thus, when she made the Church her hallowed shrine,
Founded on Jesus Christ the Corner-stone,
With Prophets, and Apostles, and the Line
Of ordered Ministers, Truth ever one,
Not here or there, but in the whole hath shone.
Whilst Heresies arise of varying clime
And varying form and colour, — the true Sun,
One and the same through all advancing time,
The Whole His Mansion makes, vast, uniform sublime.

3

Mark, how each Creed stands in that Test revealed,
Romish, and Swiss, and Lutheran novelties !
As in the light of Spenser's magic shield.
Falsehood lets fall her poisoned cup and flies,
Rome's seven-headed monster sees and dies !
New forms of Schism which changing times supply,
Behold the unwonted light in wild surprise.
In darkness bold, bright-shining arms they spy,
And down their Parent's mouth the Imps of Error hie !

4

The Church her ample bosom may expand,
Again contract,—may open far and wide
Her tent, extend her cords, on either hand
Break forth, again into herself subside—;
Alike with her Faith's oracles abide,
Revered by fickle worshipper, or spurned.
Oft faint, ne'er lost, the Lamp by Heaven supplied.
Oft dimmed by envious mists, ne'er undiscerned,
God's Witness, through all time, hath in His temple burned.

5

O Holy Truth, whene'er thy voice is heard,
A thousand echoes answer to the call—;
Though oft inaudible thy gentle word,
While we regard not. Take me from the thrall
Of passionate Hopes, be thou my All in All—;
So may Obedience lead me by the hand
Into thine inner shrine and secret hall.
Thence hath thy voice gone forth o'er Sea and Land,
And all that voice may hear—but none can understand,

6

Save the obedient. From both love and hate,
Affections vile, low cares, and envy's blight,
And controversial leanings and debate,
Save me ! from earthly film my mental sight
Purge thou, make my whole body full of Light !
So may my eyes from all things Truth convey,
My ears in all thy lessons read aright,
My dull heart understand, and I obey,
Following where'er the Church hath mark'd the Ancient Way.[6]

---

6. John Henry Newman, *Lyra Apostolica* (Rivingtons, 1879), pp. 129–32.

Appendix 2

An Agenda for Us All to Follow

- To pursue the Anglican Way by upholding Canon A5 which states that the doctrine of the Church of England is grounded in the Holy Scriptures, and in such teachings of the ancient Fathers and Councils of the Church as are agreeable to the said Scriptures. In particular such doctrine is to be found in the Thirty-nine Articles of Religion, the Book of Common Prayer and the Ordinal.

- To promote the conception of the Church which we have inherited, founded by the Lord Himself, perpetuated by direct succession from the Apostles, one in continuous history and in doctrine with the Primitive Church, filled with a supernatural and sacramental life, witnessing to a high moral standard before the world. To work for the reinstatement of discipline and doctrine in the prevailing secularisation and dysfunctioning of the Church of England and the Anglican Communion.

- To assert the reality of the Church as a spiritual body perpetuated by the Apostolic Succession recognising that we have received our Church from the Apostles as a divine inheritance and conveying life through its Sacraments – this as against the innovations of the liberals reflected in the pervasive humanism and apostasy in the Church and sometimes supported in Parliament.

- To assert the authoritative doctrinal character of our Anglican Formularies as against the liberalism so often evident in the deliberations and policies of the General Synod.
- To recall Anglicans to the revival of neglected truth and 'principles of action which had been in the minds of our predecessors of the seventeenth century'. As the Oxford Fathers urged 'Stir up the gift of God that is in you'.
- To uphold and elucidate the doctrines of the Catholic Faith as Anglicans have received them and to work for the expression of such doctrine by the avoidance of the dumbing-down effect of the language of 'political correctness' in liturgy and biblical translations.
- To resist today's new insidious Erastianism, the interference of the government in the affairs of the Church, whereby a government can dictate to the Church what its doctrine and morality should be as a result of various types of discriminatory law.
- To work for the unity in truth and holiness of all Christians and as Anglicans to bring our own characteristic contribution as our fathers have taught us, according to the Apostolic Doctrine and Polity of our Church.
- To bring recognition to the reality that the way of salvation is the partaking of the Body and Blood of our sacrificed Redeemer by means of the Holy Sacrament of the Eucharist and that the security for the due application of this is the Apostolic Commission. We cannot and do not accept therefore the innovation of women priests and women bishops since Sacraments are from God and we cannot tamper with them. The Sacraments must never be humanly manipulated on the basis of the politico-sociological arguments of the times and so-called 'human rights.'

- To be on our watch for all opportunities of inculcating a due sense of this inestimable privilege; to provide and circulate information, to familiarise the imaginations of people with the idea; to attempt to revive among churchmen the practice of daily common prayer and the more frequent participation in the Eucharist.

- To urge the bishops and clergy to a fuller realisation of their divine gift of Holy Order as successors of the Apostles and ordained ministers. To promote the lawful establishment of a free, additional, non-territorial Third Province, the case for which and the means of achieving it are set out both theologically and legally in *Consecrated Women?*[1] It is in this that these principles can be given their due application.

Conclusion

In the spirit of John Henry Newman, the aim is not the seeking of our own well-being, or originality, or some new invention for the Church. Let our prayer be that God will give us sound judgement, patient thought, discrimination, a comprehensive mind, and abstinence from all private fancies and caprices and personal tastes.[2] Let us seek only the standards of saintliness and service as the measure of our activities.

Let the secret for us lie in those words of Our Lord's High Priestly prayer, 'For their sakes I consecrate myself', so uniting His humanity with God in the way of holiness that He may capture the reality of that life within the Blessed Trinity and be inspired by the divine life He lives with God in the Holy Spirit. For it is only as we make

[1.] J. Baker (ed.) *Consecrated Women?* (Canterbury Press, 2004).
[2.] J. H. Newman, *Apologia*, p. 82.

our home in Him, as He made his home in the Father that we will be able to do anything.

There is the ultimate secret of power; the one sure way of doing good in our generation. We cannot anticipate or analyse the power of a pure and holy life; but there can be no doubt about its reality, and there seems no limit to its range. We can only know in part the laws and forces of the spiritual world; and it may be that every soul that is purified and given up to God and to His work releases or awakens energies of which we have no suspicion – energies viewless as the wind; but we can be sure of the result, and we may have glimpses sometimes of the process.

Surely, there is no power in the world so unerring or as irrepressible as the power of personal holiness. All else at times goes wrong, blunders, loses proportion, falls disastrously short of its aim, grows stiff or one-sided, or out of date – 'whether there be prophesies they shall fail; whether there be tongues, they shall cease; whether there be knowledge, it shall vanish away'; but nothing mars or misleads the influence that issues from a pure and humble and unselfish character.

A man's gifts may lack opportunity, his efforts may be misunderstood and resisted; but the spiritual power of a consecrated will needs no opportunity, and can enter where the doors are shut. By no fault of a man's own, his gifts may suggest to some the thoughts of criticism, comparison, competition; his self-consecration can do no harm in this way. Of gifts, some are best for long distances, some for objects close at hand or in direct contact; but personal holiness, determining, refining, characterising everything that a man says or does, will tell alike on those he may not know even by name, and on those who see him in the constant intimacy of his home.'[3]

[3.] Francis Paget, 'The Hallowing of Work', cited in A. W. Robinson, *The Personal Life of the Clergy*, (Longmans Green and Co., 1902), pp. 17–18.

An Afterword

When this book first appeared a bishop wrote to thank me for writing it, saying that the Anglican mind is precisely what many in the Anglican communion are determined to repudiate, and permanently so. Some are even determined to repudiate the Christian mind. There was a belief before July 2008 that General Synod would provide the kind of legislation that would enable those opposed to women bishops to remain respected members of the Church of England; a separate jurisdiction enshrined in law. Against the advice of the Archbishops, the judgement of the Manchester Group set up to advise it, the pleas of most senior bishops, and contrary to its own earlier resolutions, the Synod voted against making any proper provision for traditionalists. In the vindictive spirit of that July Synod where politics supplanted the Faith of the Church, sadly, the Synod mindset fired by an unfeminine militancy would make no concessions for the unity of the Church. The spirit of Our Lord's prayer 'that they may all be one' was absent.

The unity of the Church whether it be, Eastern, Western or our own, was missing from the mind of the proponents of women bishops when it should have been their first priority. Sadly, it has never been given any priority in the debate about the feminizing of Holy Order. Every attempt to make it a priority, whether from within the Church of England, or from outside, has always been rejected. At a meeting between the Pope and the Archbishop of Canterbury in November 2006, both acknowledged that serious obstacles remain to unity between the Roman Catholic Church and the Anglican Church. Both agreed that disagreements on the ordination of gay bishops and women priests and the blessing of same-sex unions were serious obstacles. Similarly the Greek Orthodox and Russian Orthodox through their patriarchs have warned against these innovations. Since this debate began, the exclusion of women from Holy Order has been seen as discrimination, a word that has become a contemporary political term now used in the sense of prejudice and unfairness in the secular world and so an infringement of human rights. In 'my kingdom' that 'is not of this world' 'discrimination' is the making of a discerning distinction and Jesus did this in the choosing of men for the apostolic ministry.

As mentioned earlier,[1] in 'Of Ceremonies' the *Book of Common Prayer* states that 'the wilful and contemptuous transgression and breaking of a common order and discipline is no small offence before God ... therefore no man ought to take in hand, nor presume to appoint or alter any publick or common Order in Christ's Church, except he be lawfully called and authorized thereunto.' Ignatius of Antioch wrote to the Ephesians, 'I exhort you to be in harmony with the thought of God; for Jesus Christ, our inseparable life, is the Father's thought ... hence it is right for you to be in harmony with the thought of God ...' When episcopacy was being threatened by Presbyterians in Ireland, Sir George Radcliffe wrote to John Bramhall (1594–1663) that a constant succession from the Apostles

---

[1] p. 17

with sole power to give orders appropriate to them and none other is what makes a Bishop according to the practice of the Catholic Church and the authority of the most ancient Councils. All other ordinations are not irregular only, but void. '... nothing can make a Priest, or a Bishop, but authority from Heaven, without which all successions and ordinations are not only uncanonical but mere nullities.'[2] This is no more or less than Hooker. The feminising of Holy Order is based on the secular arguments of political correctness and human rights so that such people will have the superintendence but not the sacramental character of Holy Order. In *Anglicans and the Future* Bishop Michael Ramsey said 'Towards one another as Anglicans our unity will be one of giving and receiving ... towards other Churches we work for truth and holiness ... what we may give is not our own, it is a treasure of scriptural and catholic faith and sacrament. As to the goal, it is nothing less than full communion in and of the Catholic Church of Christ'. Also, that any true development must bear witness to the Gospel, express the general consciousness of Christians and serve the organic unity of the Church in all its parts. This is classical Anglican divinity, that we should not, for the sake of local unity, do anything that would be an obstacle to the re-integration of the Church in East and West.

The Bishop of Manchester, chairman of the Manchester Commission stated in Crux, his diocesan monthly, that 'The ways of General Synod – especially in these sorts of debates – do not easily allow for subtle exploration or diplomatic conclusion.' He went on to say that the report asked the General Synod to consider what kind of Church it wanted to be. He concluded that there was little

---

2. The Rawdon Papers, L xxxvii, p. 95, 1643, cited in *John Bramhall* by Sparrow Simpson [SPCK, 1927], pp. 67–68.

evidence during the debate that the question about the future nature of our Church was being addressed or even understood. The Bishop of Durham, who had called for a postponement of the debate welcomed the Bishop of Manchester's comments and described the Synod as a 'blunt instrument'. The issue highlighted by the Archbishop of Canterbury was not just about what we decide but how we decide. The Bishop of Blackburn called for clarification between Synod and episcopacy and stated that Synod is 'totally out of control.' He rejected the parliamentary model of General Synod and saw the role of the bishops as being present to listen and then leave and make decisions. The votes of clergy and laity should be used as information for the bishops to act on.[3]

The spirit of the Synod debate was nasty and intolerant, even refusing to make room for the expressed wishes of senior churchmen. It revealed the ugly character of the feminists in their avowed resolve to dominate the Church. Some Synod members were in tears in the face of such uncharitableness, one bishop even saying he was 'ashamed' of the Church of England. It revealed a lack of awareness of, even an unbelief in, Anglican Church principles and revealed an agenda that is dedicated to subverting the institution and turning it into its opposite. This apostasy of our time that rejects the apostolic tradition of its founding Scriptures means that Anglicanism is losing its authenticity as a Church. The proponents of women bishops have made it an issue of gender, equality and justice rather than an ecclesiological matter and this has made it impossible to have a theological discussion. Furthermore, it is based on the fundamental error that male and female are interchangeable rather than complementary. Directly linked with this is the issue of same-sex

---

[3.] *C of E Newspaper*, 3 October 2008, by Michael Brown and Toby Cohen

blessings and while Anglicans are being encouraged to see both issues as 'secondary' issues, the Church of Rome and Orthodoxy see them as of the first order. They are not primarily a matter of human rights and inclusion but symptoms of a fundamental misunderstanding of the Doctrines of Creation and Redemption. Implementing such innovations on the basis of a misreading of the truth of the created and redemptive orders is a gigantic mistake that blurs our focus, diverts us from fulfilling God's will and raises another obstacle to the unity of the Church in East and West. It is not the following of Christ but the supplanting of a man-centred ideology to tell him where he went wrong.

Fourteen bishops responded to General Synod's decision and wrote to fourteen hundred clergy, who, before Synod, had written to the Archbishops of Canterbury and York resolving to leave the Church of England if the Synod voted in favour of women bishops with no provision for opponents. They expressed sympathy and understanding of the difficulties we are all facing in the light of the instruction by General Synod to the Manchester Group to prepare legislation with only a statutory code of practice for the opponents of women bishops with theological objections in the absence of wider Catholic consensus. No code of practice can deliver the necessary ecclesial provision, and the bishops want the Manchester Group and the House of Bishops to be in no doubt about the seriousness of the situation. Also, it is important to acknowledge that it is not clear that the House of Laity would support legislation whose inevitable consequence would exclude substantial numbers of faithful Anglicans from the Church of England.'

For the fourteen bishops leaving the Church of England is not an option because of the encouragement of friends in the other historic churches to continue to struggle for the catholic identity of Anglicanism. The aim of the letter was to assure priests that these bishops are working to ensure that the Church of England secures an honoured place for the opponents of women bishops as General Synod promised in the early 1990s. Faithfulness to the ARCIC vision of full visible unity was affirmed as an Anglican commitment. Many people, including bishops, who do not agree with us about women bishops, do not want to see the exclusion of our contribution from the ongoing life of the Church of England.

Responses from other Bishops

The Bishop of Rochester, Dr Michael Nazir-Ali, speaking to the Prayer Book Society AGM warned that the Anglican Church was too ready to adapt to modern culture. He called for the Church to reaffirm its traditional identity as a confessing, conciliar and consistory church. He was also critical of councils that 'make no decisions', a veiled attack on the recent Lambeth Conference.[4]

The Bishop of Durham, Dr Tom Wright, wrote in a letter to his clergy to stress how unclear everything still is and to say he does not believe this is an issue over which we should divide the Church. The Lambeth Conference and our other Instruments of Communion have said there must be room for both opinions on this matter, and the Church of England made promises in the early 1990s, which I do not believe we should break. 'There are many of you in this diocese and elsewhere who are enormously valued members of our team and I want to continue to work with you to find ways forward.'

Bishop John Broadhurst of Fulham said 'The General

[4.] Reported in *The Times* by Ruth Gledhill 14 September 2008

Synod is ... presuming to decide doctrine separate from
the tradition, separate from scripture, separate from the
universal brief and practice of the Church. This is not a
vote we have lost ... this is human beings presuming to
tell God in Jesus Christ he got it wrong, presuming to tell
the majority of Christians we know better.' He urged
people not to leave the Church as the outcome of the
dispute could still be changed.[5] Legally it is possible to re-
introduce matters that have already been rejected even at
the risk of a second rejection by Synod, but if the bishops
could unite around something possible the Synod might
accept it. Furthermore there has not been a rush to Rome,
nor serious calls to abandon ship. Clergy and laity are
continuing as before to worship and pray as members of
the Church of England. We are not 'threatening to leave'
as opponents suggested but promising to stay. 'We are
reliably assured that at least three of the diocesan bishops
who have hitherto been of the opposite persuasion have
"crossed the floor" in the wake of what happened at
York.'[6]

Also, lay opposition is growing, and while the figures
are insignificant at this stage it must be a worrying and
unexpected trend for those wanting total victory. Synod
figures show 32% against in 2005, 36% in 2006 and 38% in
2008, which makes no difference at this stage, where only
simple majorities are required in the initial votes. If the
trend continues, however, at the final and decisive stage in
2014, there could be a real possibility that the necessary
two-thirds majority might not be achieved among the
laity. So a decade's work in Synod could be destroyed.

[5.] Address to National Assembly of Forward in Faith, 11 October 2008
[6.] Anglican Association Minutes 13 August 2008

On the wider constitutional front,

> ... liberal elements within the Church of England ... by asserting the validity of the ordination of women in the Church will eventually undermine episcopacy and the monarchy. After all: 'In the seventeenth century, the equation "no bishop, no king" proved to be true when the Presbyterian attack on episcopacy led to the fall of the monarchy. Today the formula is "no priest, no bishop, no king".' The radical secularisation of Britain which would follow disestablishment would endanger rather than preserve religious liberty in this country, as Non-Conformist, Roman Catholic and Jewish leaders (who are not seeking to cut the link between Church and State) are acutely aware. It would also force the monarchy to operate in a secular milieu and to be appraised in a strictly functional manner, for which it is ill-suited. It would only be a matter of time before the Sovereign was replaced as head of state by an elected president (probably a failed politician) as part of a grandiose scheme for constitutional reform.[7]

A group of ordinands from St Stephen's House, Oxford, have written to the House of Bishops telling them that it is the responsibility of the bishops to 'lead us from the brink of irreparable damage to the systems of government within the Church of England, and now is the time to do it. ... it is possible for the House of Bishops to provide the leadership and unity that is so urgently needed on this matter.'[8]

Evangelicals have not remained unaffected by Synod's decision and Reform[9] sees now the women-bishop issue as being urgent and the need of their constituency for a separate English bishop because of the Church's liberal direction on women bishops and homosexuality. The

---

[7.] Charles Douglas-Home, *Dignified and Efficient*, Claridge Press 2001, pp. 220-21
[8.] *Open Letter to the House of Bishops*, 13/11/08
[9.] October 2008 Conference 2008

Revd Rod Thomas, chairman of Reform said, 'we are actively going to take forward the agenda of alternative episcopal oversight. We are no longer able to sit back and wait to see what happens.' Their need is for Episcopal oversight of a bishop who shares their beliefs in tradition and the Bible. The hope is to find an English solution and avoid the litigious road of the American Episcopal Church, but it may mean parishes ceasing to identify themselves with the Church of England, and identifying instead with the global 'fellowship of confessing Anglicans' established in Jerusalem in 2008 (GAFCON). Evangelicals are being encouraged to mobilize themselves to take over the General Synod by getting elected.

GAFCON

The idea of a decade of evangelism was proposed by the African bishops at the 1988 Lambeth Conference. These same bishops safeguarded the Communion's orthodox teaching on marriage and sexuality at the 1998 Lambeth Conference that issued in resolution 1.10. In the ensuing years these orthodox primates ensured that the primates' meetings and the Anglican Consultative Council stood by this resolution. What came to be called Global South orthodox Anglicans were the prime movers in calling for order and discipline. After the Dar-es-Salaam primates' meeting that went against Archbishop Rowan's wishes there were no subsequent meetings, and they were not consulted about invitations to Lambeth. When they realised that they were not being listened to and their pleas to postpone Lambeth were ignored, while decisions were not being acted upon, they concluded that they must act and define what Anglicanism is. It was the decision to invite the consecrators of the practising homosexual bishop Gene Robinson that triggered their decision. So before Lambeth 2008 came the GAFCON conference and subsequently the Jerusalem Statement and Declaration 'which defined global identity as a matter of orthodox and biblically faithful belief.'

The Jerusalem Declaration is a declaration of fellowship that states the basis of fellowship and communion among Anglicans in terms of Anglican identity. Anglican identity is shaped by commitment to Canon A5:

> The doctrine of the Church is grounded in the Holy Scriptures and in such teachings of the ancient Fathers and Councils of the Church as are agreeable to the said Scriptures. In particular, such doctrine is to be found in the Thirty-nine Articles of Religion, the Book of Common Prayer and the Ordinal.

This is a different emphasis from the way pursued by Lambeth where the 'instruments of communion' give the impression that communion arises institutionally, and that questions of communion are therefore dealt with through those instruments of communion, the Archbishop of Canterbury and the Anglican Consultative Council. Anglican identity then becomes an institutional question – except that these instruments have failed to deliver for more than a decade. The Jerusalem Declaration reminds us that our own canons are on a different wave-length and tell us that fellowship arises out of a common confession, out of one faith. It is a consequence of our unity in One Lord, one faith, one baptism that Ephesians 4.5 speaks of.

To ground Anglican fellowship in Scripture and Creed, the teaching of the ancient Councils and the Book of Common Prayer has consequences on how irregularities in doctrine and morals are viewed. Such irregularities in the departure from Scripture and tradition in North America are viewed very differently by someone who sees the bonds of fellowship as primarily institutional, arising from the determination to keep the structures from breaking. Also, viewed differently is the crossing of diocesan or provincial boundaries of jurisdiction. As stated earlier[10] there is ancient precedent for this practice, for the geographical principle is valid but not paramount and is designed to serve the Gospel priorities as defined in Scripture. It ceases to be valid and needs displacement when it contradicts those scriptural imperatives. The Jerusalem Declaration endorses this ancient precedent.

In these two views of fellowship, the confessional and the institutional, each is not exclusively so. The institutional is concerned for confessional questions and the confessional is concerned for institutional matters. The difference lies in the order of priority given to each of these matters that is determined by the different conceptions of Anglican identity, and this will affect how we respond to the oppressive and marginalizing treatment of orthodox Anglicans in other Provinces. Should they toe the institutional line, or get out, or fight to preserve an Anglican identity that is consistent with Scripture and Tradition? Surely Canon A5 is our historical compass to justify the preservation of the apostolic origin of our Anglican identity.

Lambeth 2008

It is too early to evaluate how Anglican history will assess Lambeth 2008 – a Conference from which two hundred and thirty bishops absented themselves. The reason for their absence was the Archbishop of Canterbury acting

---

[10.] chapter 2 page 23

alone, issuing invitations to Lambeth 2008 in July 2007 without the Primates' meeting and before the TEC had formally responded to the Dar-es-Salaam communiqué or the Primates had been able to evaluate the TEC response. 'How can we explain to our church members' they said, 'that while we and they are formally out of communion with the Episcopal Church of America, we at the same time live with them at the Lambeth Conference as though nothing had happened? This would be hypocrisy.' Another reason for non-attendance was because the Archbishop of Canterbury had invited the consecrators of the divorced, practising homosexual bishop Gene Robinson. Some bishops attended GAFCON and Lambeth, but 29% of the Communion's bishops absented themselves from a conference whose controlling framework was the liberal world view of always being on a journey and therefore unable to provide answers. As Canon Chris Sugden pointed out,

> ... they want all views present, but those with orthodox views are asked to sit with those who preach heresy. This is like asking for a consultation about a patient afflicted with a devastating illness to include both those who come from the long experience of medical science, and practitioners of alternative medicine in all its forms.[11]

The chairman of the Bible Study Committee, Gerald West admitted being non-committal on Lambeth 1.10. He is the author of a *Gay Primer* for the Church of South Africa. So as Archbishop Orombi wrote,[12] 'We believe that our absence at this Lambeth Conference is the only way that our voice will be heard. For more than ten years we have been speaking and have not been heard. So maybe our

---

11. Lambeth Conference News 11 November 2008
12. in *The Times* (August 1st)

absence will speak louder than our words.' Even during the conference some orthodox primates and bishops distanced themselves and did not receive Holy Communion and missed some of their *Indaba* sessions, *Indaba* being a Zulu style of meeting to discuss and deal with problems. In a conference that acknowledged the existence of deep crisis in the Anglican Communion but was so stage-managed as to avoid discussion of it or the finding of a solution for it. The term *Indaba* was misused because the meetings were designed to reach no particular conclusions, solutions or resolutions for action. When asked about an emergent agenda the Archbishop of Canterbury referred to the statement of the Windsor Continuation Group that had called for a complete cessation of blessings for same-sex unions, the consecrations of practising homosexuals and lesbians and the 'cross-border interventions and inter-provincial claims of jurisdiction.' This is merely a repetition of what Primates' meetings have requested in 2003, 2005 and 2007, that the Windsor Group admitted had been 'less than wholeheartedly embraced on all sides ... The failure to respond presents us with a situation where if all three moratoria are not observed the Communion is likely to fracture.' The Fellowship of Confessing Anglican Primates have admitted that this cannot work and that the Communion is at the brink of collapse but within GAFCON they look forward to cooperation in the future to avoid such collapse and work to renew the Communion.

Canon Sugden has pointed out[13] that the culture of Lambeth was of Inclusive Church, of diversity in unity where most self-select sessions were from the liberal perspective and the marketplace dominated by gay organisations. In his second presidential address the Arch-

---

13. Ibid

bishop expressed the hope 'that we speak from the centre. We should try to speak from the heart of our identity as Anglicans; and ultimately from that deepest centre which is our awareness of living in and as the Body of Christ.' Sugden has asked what the heart of our identity as Anglicans is. Is it defined by the faith, or is it defined by inclusion? Traditional Anglican liberalism was based on Christian truths, but secular liberalism denies that truth is possible and urges the equality of every person and their views. Secular liberalism places the value of inclusion over against faithfulness and faith. But as Sugden pointed out 'The claim to speak from the centre must face the challenge of whether the faith that defines the centre is the centre of faith, or the centre of the secular vision of inclusion?' John Richardson[14] pointed out, despite Lambeth *Reflections*, 'only the pathologically optimistic will suppose anything is going to deter the western churches from promoting and supporting the revisionist agenda ... the dominant voice on campus, other than the bishops themselves, was that of the many pro-LGBT groups, not only in the marketplace but via a daily "newspaper".'

Retrieving our own Household Riches

Two people who were among those to receive a copy of *Restoring the Anglican Mind* were Cardinals Kasper and Dias. We cannot assume they read it, but in what they said at the Lambeth Conference there are echoes of convergence with its message. Cardinal Dias warned that the real danger in Western Christianity is the religious equivalent of amnesia 'when we live myopically in the fleeting

---

[14.] *New Directions* (September 2008)

present, oblivious of our past heritage and apostolic traditions.' It results in disorderly behaviour, a dysfuntionalism without 'any coordination with the head or the other members of our community' and produces ecclesial paralysis. Cardinal Kasper spoke to the Lambeth Conference of his desire to see Anglicanism recover its classical Anglican divinity as displayed in the Caroline divines and the Tractarians. In those critical times Anglicans retrieved the strength of the Church of the Fathers when that tradition was in jeopardy.

> Perhaps in our own day it would be possible too, to think of a new Oxford Movement, a retrieval of riches which lay within your own household. This would be a re-reception, a fresh recourse to the Apostolic Tradition in a new situation. It would not mean a renouncing of your deep attentiveness to human challenges and struggles, your desire for human dignity and justice, your concern with the active role of all women and men in the Church. Rather, it would bring these concerns and the questions that arise from them more directly within the framework shaped by the Gospel and ancient common tradition in which our dialogue is grounded.

The question

Thirty years ago Michael Ramsey was advocating the need for a new Oxford Movement. It is an attractive proposition and invites a discerning consideration, not in the sense of replicating a piece of past history which would be impossible, but in a discernment of what the essence of that Movement was and the underlying principles that motivated it. The Tractarians' concern was why the Church was so weak in the face of the dangers which threatened it; dangers from the outside but also in the actual life of the Church of their day. William Palmer said, that such enemies were seeking the subversion of the Church's essential characteristics. For such people the Church was no more than an association for the promotion of religion and social virtue. Matters of dogmatic belief, ecclesiastical organization and liturgical observance were only of secondary importance. Hence the Church lacked that clear principle by which it could define its true character and defend itself against the world. So national apostasy and ecclesiastical apostasy were two sides of the same coin.

Our question is the same; does the Anglican Church have a distinctive and independent witness to the society in which it is set, or is it to be 'conformed to this world', or is its purpose to be very much more?

Today's apostasy

Reports, pronouncements, actions, and people wheeled in front of TV cameras today, generally reflect a vague liberal consensus, a desperate chasing after trendiness and a feeling that change is good for its own sake. Ecumenism has become wishy-washy and much practical religion no more than a sentimental projection of the feel-good factor with à la carte choices, a Rocky Horror religion that is simply wrong and bogus and about adapting religion to a lifestyle rather than vice-versa. In General Synod and elsewhere, not only is there an ignorance of theology and our Anglican heritage but a rejection of it. Peter Hitchens wrote in *The Daily Mail*, that the real issue is the presence of radical reformers in the Church, whose principles they don't support, in order to change it into something else. They are uncharitable, intolerant of opposition and actively hope to drive others out of the Church they love. Their opponents are made to look like narrow-minded bigots because they are permanently on the defensive in their fight over issues that can easily be misrepresented to outsiders. It reminds us

of the religious temper of the age that faced the Tractarians.
Today's apostasy is as real as what Keble preached
against. It intrudes itself as political correctness that is
tearing the Anglican Communion apart in the struggle of
two incompatible religions. Its aim is to re-interpret biblical and credal orthodoxy by means of a sociological reduc-
tionism and conform it to the secular spirit of the age.

Episcopal Office

The bishops in their lives and teaching do not exemplify
their status and function as the apostolic ministry in and to
the Church founded by Christ. This is reduced to a func-
tionalism that anyone can do; man or woman. An understanding of the Episcopal office is missing in the
contemporary Church of England and this is why there is
so much confusion over it, even among bishops, and why
it is so difficult to get across its absolute centrality for the
Church in reunion discussions. A want of principle
prevents that re-appraisal of the Episcopal order, vital for
our Church, a principle by which we can assess and
reform. The Tractarians missed it too, they point us to the
need for a recovery of emphasis on the Apostolic Succession and the sacramental character of the episcopate. They
sought to revive an awareness of the true character of the
bishop, and of the fact that this character was the most
important thing about him. It was the symbol of the divine
origin of the whole Church.

Priesthood

Also, the Tractarians were concerned with the renewal of
the priesthood by their emphasis on sacramental and

priestly ideals, changing the whole character of priestly ministry and awakening the clergy with their watch-cry, 'Stir up the gift that is in you.' Renewal in our Church must begin, as did the Oxford Movement, though not of course end, with the renewal of the priesthood.

Returning to prescriptive sources

The Tractarians were concerned for a return to the prescriptive sources of Anglicanism. As already pointed out we must make friends with the great Anglican divines of the seventeenth century and the early Christian Fathers that were the bedrock of their theology. This is vital for the renewal of the Church and also for the intellectual and spiritual formation and nourishment of the clergy. For the Tractarians a priest's life and work must be grounded in sound doctrine, the traditional and orthodox faith of the Church, which rested for them on the Bible, the early Fathers, the Book of Common Prayer and the Anglican divines of the 17th century. Such studies must be the bulwark to protect the Church's faith from those foes within and without; those people who would water it down and conform it to a secular society's values. How many priests know the Fathers or anything in their own classical Anglican tradition where there are crucial resources for their intellectual and devotional life? How much is today's ordinand informed of these resources in theological college? The evidence suggests that emphasis is more heavily weighted on the agenda of politically correct issues than classical Anglican theology, and a liberal imperialism dominates. Here in our own household are rich resources to nourish clergy and laity in an Anglican orthodoxy.

Our Church and its leaders apparently are not presenting a vigorous and reasoned defence of those core doctrines which are the Church's foundation; doctrines and sacramental life not our own but received from the universal Church. We need to be made aware of the spiritual treasures of the Anglican divines who preserved the Reformed and Catholic heritage of the Church of England; and whose heirs the Tractarians recognized themselves to be. Once more, Anglican renewal must have its theological side; a re-statement and affirmation of the Church's historic faith in this twenty-first century. There is little sign of this as yet. These divines have much to say to us of the whole tenor and temper of modern church life. They saw the Christian life in terms of holiness, the sanctity of the individual member and the whole body of the faithful. Theology is not just a matter of intellectual clarity but the union of human lives with God in the way of holiness. So the Christian life is 'one of constant discipline where we are immersed in holy things which are to be handled in a spirit of sobriety, austerity and awe.' This is such a contrast to the loss of dignity in the casualness and laid-back mateyness of much Christian worship today. For these divines the Church is a supernatural body that reflects the divine holiness and this present life is a preparation for the life to come. The 'life of the world to come' is not merely in the future but it is a present eternal state that penetrates our earthly life.

Christopher Howse[15] in an article 'Anglicans who've lost their memory' quotes the historian Jonathan Clarke who claims that Anglicanism is 'losing command of its history', thus losing its identity that is akin to losing one's memory. The professor states that in the twentieth century Anglicanism was powered by German theology rather than by Anglican historiography and this has resulted in a

---

15. *The Daily Telegraph* 22 November 2008

loss of authority which is 'ultimately historically grounded.' This is the reason why feminism and gay rights have come to preoccupy so much of the attention of Anglicans. The irony is that 'at the moment when the Church of England is losing its historical sense of identity it should be led by an Archbishop of Canterbury with a profound knowledge of history.' One of the causes of this discontinuity is the neglect of the teaching of its history and a lack of concern for the fate of its ancient libraries and a resistance to promoting scholarly clergy. Another cause promoted by some historically aware Anglicans is the depiction of the Church of England 'as essentially a radical Protestant denomination with a revolutionary foundation in the early 16th century.' One of the results has been the marginalizing of Catholics over the ordination of women.

The Aftermath of the General Synod

After the July 2008 Synod the outlook looks dark but not hopeless. If it seems that the English Catholic Church is disappearing into sectarianism; remember that it is still present in us. If we are in a New Interregnum then we must realise that we cannot survive by a policy of mere aloofness and obstruction. We must continue to justify our opposition on theological and historical grounds and so inform ourselves to do so. Our encouragement of others can create a renewal of Anglican theology and priesthood in a defence of Anglicanism that must be intellectually sound. Our aim and that of our constituency must be to build an edifice of reasoned theology and devotion in support of orthodox Anglican Church principles. Not only will this moderate our opponents. It will make these principles intelligible to them. This need is crucially urgent when so many theological schemes for training priests have retreated from theology. We must encourage our ordinands and laity to engage with us in this endeavour by organising groups and conferences and providing the necessary resources. From lectures and retreats I have given, I am conscious of clergy and laity here and in other parts of the world who are keen to know more about this and engage in it. Many of them have expressed a desire for an Institute of Anglican Studies located not only geographically in world-wide branches but also in cyber-space to provide resources to inform them in the restoring of the Anglican mind and to network orthodox Anglicans for the mutual support of each other. This would be supportive of such Anglicans who find themselves isolated and without any jurisdictional protection and threatened by those trying to marginalise them and exclude them from the Church. Also, it would build up a world-wide constituency of orthodox Anglicans.

Let us avoid knee-jerk reactions of rushing into the arms of another Communion, or becoming a defeated and bedraggled remnant begging Rome for ecclesiastical asylum. Let us continue to stand firm in our Anglican orthodoxy against the modernism that is doing its worst to conform our Church to secularism. Let us reach out to Evangelicals whose concern is for a biblical and historical Anglican orthodoxy and then we will have the riches of our Anglican patrimony to bring into a reunited Church. In this spirit we can take up the challenge of Cardinal Kasper, to retrieve the riches which lie within our own household and retrieve the strength of the Church of the Fathers, a fresh recourse to the Apostolic Tradition in a new situation.

Printed in the United Kingdom
by Lightning Source UK Ltd.
135931UK00001B/235-318/P